PRAISE FOR *PATH TO*

Early in Carolyn Butler-Madden's *Path to Purpose*, the author reflects on a simple human truth: that we all want to contribute positively to this world. 'We just need to be shown a way that we can do it easily.' The book that follows is a refreshingly straightforward almanac of great value to any business seeking to align its strategy with its *raison d'être*, while making it easy for audiences to jump aboard.

Butler-Madden brings an astute and compelling perspective to why cause-driven business is good business, why ethics are an increasingly critical factor in corporate success and how businesses that engage authentically with audiences through shared values can build and accelerate their brands in the process.

The well-researched blend of international and Australian cases featured is impressive for the fact that despite the variety of causes pursued – diversity, gender equality, fair trade, cancer research, world hunger, refugee support and others – there are some universal principles at work behind purpose-driven businesses.

From Cricket Australia's Pink Test to Allstate's Purple Purse program, from Patagonia to Pampers, *Path to Purpose* reveals the galvanising energy of cause marketing. It also supports the proposition that brand-building actually becomes easier when purpose-driven, with so many willing audience participants motivated by the desire to participate.

To Marketing 101's hackneyed 'Seven Ps', Butler-Madden's book implies we must now add an eighth: Purpose – the most critical driver of corporate sustainability and success. As the author notes, 'Marketers need to think less about what their brands can say about themselves, and more about what their brands can do for the world we live in.' Amen to that.

David Redhill, Partner, Global Chief Marketing Officer, Deloitte Consulting

We live in a world craving meaningful connection that comes from meaningful communication. Carolyn Butler-Madden understands this better than most and that's what makes her exceptional book, *Path to Purpose*, so incredibly valuable for anyone wanting to build a powerful brand in the modern world.

Andrew Griffiths, International Bestselling Author, Speaker, Global Presenter, Media Commentator

An ever-increasing number of brands are linking purchase to purpose. They are understanding that when their brand plays a more meaningful role in society it unites people towards their brands in a truly positive and profitable way. Brands that just 'say and pray' are the brands of the past. Brands that 'do' around a clearly defined purpose are the growth engines of the future.

David Fox, Chief Executive Officer, Ogilvy Group Australia

Path to Purpose is a great addition to the small library of books containing the insights professionals need to create initiatives that successfully do well by doing good. It's especially exciting to have access to its collection of Australian case studies. Bravo and thanks Carolyn Butler-Madden!

David Hessekiel, Founder and President, Cause Marketing Forum, Inc.

I'm a believer in the power of local communities and social movements to change the world. Every now and again you get the chance to meet and work with people who you know are going to lead this change in a new and exciting direction.

PATH TO PURPOSE

HOW TO USE **CAUSE MARKETING** TO BUILD A MORE MEANINGFUL AND PROFITABLE BRAND

CAROLYN BUTLER-MADDEN

First published in 2017 by Major Street Publishing Pty Ltd
E   info@majorstreet.com.au
W   majorstreet.com.au
M   +61 421 707 983

ORDERING INFORMATION

Quantity sales. Special discounts are available on quantity purchases by corporations, associations and others. For details, contact the author.

The moral rights of the author have been asserted

National Library of Australia Cataloguing-in-Publication entry

Creator: Butler-Madden, Carolyn, author.
Title: Path to purpose: how to use cause marketing to build a more meaningful and profitable brand/Carolyn Butler-Madden.
ISBN: 9780648087502 (paperback)
Subjects: Branding (Marketing) – Australia.
Brand name products – Australia.
Marketing – Management.

Internal design by Production Works
Cover design by Ed Balila
Printed in Australia by SOS Media

10 9 8 7 6 5 4 3 2 1

To Siena, Gany and Wilma.
For your patience, support and love
— thank you.

Carolyn is not just a believer, she's out there leading the charge of an exciting movement where people and brands do well by doing good. This book is for anyone who believes that passion and authenticity don't just have a role, but should be centre-stage in business.

Graham West, National President, St Vincent de Paul Society, Honorary Fellow, Macquarie University and Not-For-Profit Consultant

Carolyn's passion for purpose marketing shines through clearly in this text. She is not only a believer but an experienced practitioner in this area and has been able to share this passion in clearly laid out chapters with tips and hints and invaluable case studies. Through experience working with Carolyn I know that she puts these words into action in her work. This book is a must-read for modern marketers looking for authentic and enduring relationships with their customers.

Mark Leathan, Product, Brand and Communication Marketing Specialist

We can transform our simple purchase act into a power of good by choosing a brand that leverages its marketing muscles and social media outreach to make a positive impact to social and environmental issues. This in turn creates more connections with the brand and more business. Winning brands will be the ones that can do good while doing well.

Nada Dugas, Senior Communication Executive, Public-Private Partnerships Builder

I think that business leaders actually already know that purpose is an imperative. In my job though, I see them struggle constantly with the practicalities of implementing a purpose-led business strategy. *Path to Purpose* provides a valuable roadmap with real life examples. This book is just the right mix of goosebumps and data to help businesses understand how leading world-change can also pay a handsome return.

Steve Matthews, Corporate Partnerships and Philanthropy Manager, Prostate Cancer Foundation of Australia

Path to Purpose is a great book that is both educational and inspirational. Not only does it cover all the basics of cause marketing, but it shares many examples of the practice that are sure to inspire you. This slim book is a wonderful read and is packed with everything you need to change the world AND grow your business. I highly recommend it!

Joe Waters, Founder and Blogger, Selfish Giving

CONTENTS

When you buy this book, something great happens

INTRODUCTION

Have you ever had goosebumps listening to a speech? I have. In 2012, I was at a cause marketing conference in Chicago listening to Nada Dugas, a senior marketer from Procter & Gamble (P&G), talk about the Pampers Nappies 'one pack = one vaccine' campaign in partnership with UNICEF. It was an extraordinary moment and one that went onto change my view of the role that brands can have in society.

Dugas had been involved in the Pampers campaign from its very early days. She talked about the impact of the campaign. Back then, in 2012, the campaign had been running for six years and had helped to eradicate Maternal and Neonatal Tetanus (MNT) in eight countries by funding over 300 million vaccines and raising over US$40 million in donations.

During her speech, Dugas highlighted that the campaign had been one of P&G's single most successful marketing campaigns globally, delivering exceptional volume and market share growth. She went on to say, with more conviction than I've heard from any marketer before or since, that P&G and Pampers would not stop in their efforts until MNT had been completely eradicated from the world. And they haven't. Today, in partnership with UNICEF, they are within a hair's breadth of achieving that outcome.

It's an incredible example of the power that brands can bring to the world today, creating much needed social impact and, in so doing, delivering the commercial outcomes that are essential to business profitability.

Pampers is just one really powerful example of a brand creating social impact and doing well as a result. There are plenty of others. There's a name for this marketing strategy. It's called cause marketing. To define it simply, it's when a brand aligns itself with a cause to drive social impact and create brand value. An authentic alignment between a brand and its selected cause partner allows the brand to develop a credible social purpose. This is then marketed in a way that enables the brand's customers, consumers, its company's employees and partners, and even the wider public, to become collaborators in creating social impact around that purpose.

Done well, it has the power to change the world.

Path to Purpose is a book written for 21st century CEOs and marketing leaders who want to build a more meaningful and purposeful brand that will thrive in a fast-changing, high demand environment.

So, let me declare my position and my credentials upfront. I have over 30 years' experience working on the agency side of marketing – first in London and then, for the last 20 years, in Australia. I have worked predominantly in below-the-line marketing and brand activation, i.e. unabashedly focusing on sales driving and engagement results. I'm particularly motivated by a desire to offer up creatively-driven solutions that deliver hardcore results. In other words, I'm not wed to being creative for the sake of creativity. For me, the end game is clear. It's about delivering tangible results.

As the marketing environment has changed over time, it's become harder to deliver those results and, like many in the industry, I've been operating in over-drive trying to figure out how to engage consumers in this new environment.

My own path to purpose came through direct experience. First, in delivering local community marketing programs for retail clients and second, by delivering cause marketing campaigns for fast-moving consumer goods (FMCGs) and retail clients. It was through these direct experiences that I realised that here was a strategy that could enable brands to genuinely connect with consumers. The early results we generated were proof of the commercial benefits – improved sales and brand health. The social benefits were also obvious as we were able to fundraise and increase awareness of the cause and the work of the cause partner.

That's when a light switched on for me and I took myself off to Chicago to the aforementioned conference to find out more about this thing called cause marketing. That conference was an eye-opener. The sophistication with which companies were leveraging this strategy was astonishing and made me realise that, in this particular area of marketing, in Australia, we might as well be living in the Dark Ages.

What bewildered me though was this: the problems that a cause or purpose-led approach solve are just as relevant to the Australian market as they are to the US and the other countries' markets, which are active in cause marketing.

If you're responsible for the marketing of a consumer-facing brand, there's a high likelihood that you are dealing with one or all of the following challenges:

1. *Brand awareness and brand health.* In today's media-fractured environment, you recognise that you need a strategy that will cut through and seize the attention of consumers, that goes beyond pricing offers and other tactical initiatives. You also understand the absolute necessity for your brand to build trust with its customers.

2. *The number crunchers need you to deliver sales today.* That focus on short-term sales makes it incredibly hard to build a brand of substance, particularly if budgets are being cut year on year.

3. *Employee engagement.* Fast becoming recognised as a crucial part of the marketing mix, most CEOs and CMOs realise that a disengaged workforce will affect customer experience, making it increasingly harder to deliver a believable brand promise.

Cause marketing is rarely considered as a marketing solution to these problems because 'cause' sits in the realm of corporate social responsibility (CSR) and is seen as a cost to business as opposed to a business opportunity. There is also a distinct lack of awareness in Australia on its successful use as a strategic marketing platform.

When cause marketing is approached strategically and executed well, it doesn't just solve one or two of the three problems highlighted above, it can solve all three of them at the same time.

This takes me back to my question of why Australian marketers are so under-informed about this particular type of marketing. Are we really so different to other markets? I don't think so. The reason I've written this book is to address this lack of awareness directly and, in doing so, to highlight the successes of both global and local brands that have used cause marketing and/or a deeper purpose-led approach.

Speaking of purpose, you may be wondering about the relationship between brand purpose and cause marketing.

Purpose has had a lot of airtime recently in marketing circles. There's no lack of information on why a brand should consider a purpose-led strategy. Despite all the chatter, there appears to be some haziness surrounding the idea of just *how* to hit the 'go' button on purpose. Inevitably, building a brand purpose is seen as a big strategic play, which for some businesses, especially in Australia's risk-averse environment, is perhaps too big and too risky.

There are a number of ways you can build a purpose-led approach for your brand. This book focuses on just one: cause marketing. It makes the simple case that, in a world where trust is the new currency and authenticity is the value by which it's judged, actions speak far louder than any words possibly can.

Cause marketing is about what your brand *does* and, just as importantly, what it enables, rather than what it *says* it is. When you take a cause marketing approach, it doesn't have to mean a complete repositioning of your brand. A cause marketing campaign can be a credible and powerful first step on a path towards purpose. For brands that already have an established brand purpose, cause marketing can also be a strong way to bring your brand purpose to life.

This book also highlights the impact that Millennials are having in driving the change in what people now expect from businesses and brands. It explains the science behind cause marketing and also makes a powerful case for why doing good is good for business.

Perhaps most important is the inspiration within these pages. Fourteen case studies, more than half of which are from Australia, will inspire you and give you confidence in exploring how cause marketing can work for your brand.

The examples come from a variety of business categories. They demonstrate the versatility of the strategy and reinforce how powerful it can be when done well.

For those of you who want to understand how to go about developing a cause marketing approach for your brand, I share my six-step methodology. It's a common sense methodology developed from my own direct experience, as well as from deconstructing cause marketing campaigns from all over the world. This methodology will enable you to:

- create a program that strategically aligns with your brand and your business's key priorities
- get support and engagement across the business and with the company's leadership team
- develop a powerful marketing platform that builds year on year
- create powerful storytelling opportunities and unlock media value beyond your dollar investment
- avoid the pitfalls associated with poorly developed or constructed cause marketing campaigns.

Central, of course, to all of this is delivering genuine social impact. This is the driving force behind every successful cause marketing campaign. When people feel a part of something important and meaningful, the effort follows, regardless of whether you're a consumer, employee, a partner or a supplier.

My hope is that once you have read this book, you'll understand why cause marketing is growing so quickly and you'll understand the power of a brand standing and acting for something and attracting followers and collaborators.

A lovely mantra that is commonly used in cause marketing circles is 'doing well by doing good'. It neatly sums up what cause marketing offers brand marketers today. And when you know how, it's really not that hard.

HOW TO GET THE MOST OUT OF *PATH TO PURPOSE*

This book has been written so that if you're unfamiliar with cause marketing and you want to read it cover to cover, you can. If time isn't on your side, or you are already familiar with the subject, I've summarised the key points at the end of each chapter. You can start with these and dive in deeper to the chapters you want more information on.

The case studies and examples are the meat in the sandwich of this book.

There are 14 case studies and they range from one-off campaign-led activities to brands that have gone on to integrate a cause or purpose into the heart of what they stand for. The shining examples will be obvious to the reader, but I encourage you to read all of them with an open mind and recognise the value that each offers – not just in creating social impact but also in getting a brand started on a path towards purpose, given that getting started is usually the hardest part of the journey.

You may notice a little bit of repetition in these pages. This is deliberate in that it enables the reader who chooses not to read the book cover to cover to get as much value from it as possible.

PART 1

DOING WELL BY DOING GOOD

CHAPTER 1

THE POWER OF PURPOSE

The Thankyou organisation is a social enterprise. You've probably heard of it. It's an Australian business with a product range including water, muesli, hand soap, body care products and, more recently, baby products. Its goal is to empower Australians and New Zealanders to make a difference in the world through making a simple choice within their everyday life – to purchase a brand that contributes to a good cause. Once all the costs of bringing Thankyou products to market are taken care of, every remaining cent funds life-changing projects in the developing world through partnerships with project-specific not-for-profit (NFP) organisations such as World Vision and the World Food Programme.

In their early days, Thankyou Water (as they were then known) had been unsuccessful in getting distribution through Coles and Woolworths. Their distribution was limited to 7-Eleven, Australia Post outlets and a network of independent supermarkets. Without the support of Coles and Woolworths, the opportunity for the organisation to fulfil its purpose was, at best, limited.

In 2013, the organisation launched a social media campaign to pressure Coles and Woolworths into stocking its range. It released a video calling on their supporters to upload videos and post comments to the Coles and Woolworths Facebook pages to show they'd buy the products if they were stocked. The Thankyou team already had a meeting scheduled with Coles, but this time they wanted to bring more than just a product to their presentation, they wanted to bring them an opportunity.

SUPPORTERS TAKE TO SOCIAL MEDIA TO CREATE OPPORTUNITY

Social media went mad. The Coles and Woolworths Facebook pages were inundated with messages and videos in the weeks leading up to the team's meeting with Coles. To support the social media campaign, the Thankyou team employed stunt tactics as helicopters flew huge banners over both retailers' head offices. An appearance on one of the main television network morning shows rounded the campaign out.

The campaign succeeded. In unleashing a torrent of public lobbying on Australia's grocery giants, Thankyou got the attention of both retailers' corporate management teams. Coles moved its scheduled meeting forward by a week and agreed to stock not only the brand's water products but also its newly launched muesli and body care range. A meeting with Woolworths ensued within the month and it too agreed to distribute the product range. Each of the retailers took 14 products from the range.

That was the breakthrough that Thankyou was looking for.

Since then, Thankyou has gone from strength to strength. In 2016, it launched into the highly competitive baby product category, as well as launching into New Zealand. It crowdfunded both of these next steps via the sale of a book about the Thankyou story. *Chapter One* was available for people to buy with the option to pay any price they wanted. Their sales target was $1.2 million. To instil a sense of urgency, a 28-day window was provided in which people were invited to buy the book. They smashed their target within the allotted time period by about $200,000. The book is still available for purchase today and as at July 2017, over 96,000 books have been sold and over $1.76 million raised.

Both of these campaigns from Thankyou are great examples of the power of purpose in unifying people behind a brand. While Thankyou is a social enterprise, it doesn't mean that traditional for-profit brands can't also benefit from an authentic purpose.

BRAND PURPOSE: START WITH 'WHY?'

As a subject, brand purpose has recently been getting more than its fair share of airtime in marketing circles. It isn't new of course but ever since Simon Sinek's TED Talk 'Start with Why' it has been highly topical. Simon Sinek simply highlighted what some brands have been doing for years – The Body Shop and Coca-Cola come to mind as very early champions of purpose, as well as Apple in more recent history.

What Sinek highlighted is that great brands sell much more than their products. Great brands have managed to understand the reason they exist beyond money and beyond product. It's a reason that never changes.

Some brands express their purpose as a mission. The semantics of the label are irrelevant. What's important is that a brand's purpose shines through and elevates it into rich emotional territory. This doesn't mean that the brand doesn't have to compete on functional benefits. Of course it does, but its purpose gives it that edge and a credibility that brands without purpose lack.

Here are some great examples of brands' purposes that will be familiar to most marketers.

Nike. 'To bring inspiration and innovation to every athlete in the world.'*

*If you have a body, you're an athlete.

Dove. 'Empower women to embrace their own beauty.'

Apple. 'To empower creative exploration and self-expression.'

Coca-Cola. 'To refresh the world... to inspire moments of optimism and happiness.'

Google. 'To organize the world's information and make it universally accessible and useful.'

Airbnb. 'To make people around the world feel like they could "belong anywhere."'

These examples show that not all brand purpose is related to causes or social responsibility. The power of any of these statements is in their value as higher order missions. They inspire people to dream. They invite people to step out of the ordinary and imagine the extraordinary. That's powerful stuff coming from a brand.

In order for purpose to be believable, there are two fundamental checkpoints that a brand needs to deliver on: credibility and authenticity. A purpose-led brand *has* to live up to its purpose. Its purpose becomes a guiding light in everything the brand does. It gives the brand immense focus and a long-term vision. It also provides a clear competitive edge against brands that focus primarily on product differentiation.

THE POWER OF PURPOSE

WHAT'S DRIVING THE MOVE TO PURPOSE-LED BRANDS?

If brand purpose isn't a new concept, why then is there so much buzz around it now? And why should marketers consider it as a strategy for their brand?

I believe a convergence of three key issues is forcing businesses, globally, to reassess their role in society.

1. Trust in corporations is rapidly declining

The 2017 Trust Barometer by global PR agency Edelman reports that trust is in crisis around the world and the results show that Australia is particularly affected. In 2016, only 52 per cent of Australians said they trusted business. A year later, that figure has fallen to 48 per cent.

Beyond the figures, everyday conversations and social media chatter highlight one striking common view – big business is greedy. Businesses don't care about their customers, their employees, their smaller business suppliers, the communities they impact, or the environment we depend on for life. They are driven by one thing and one thing only – profitability.

Whether you agree with this view of big business or not is irrelevant. The perception is there. It's deep. And it's going to be incredibly hard to shift.

2. Technology disruption: the age of the empowered consumer

Technology development has unleashed the era of consumer empowerment. People can now choose what information they receive and can filter content with controls that they've never had before. They can research and compare brands, products and services and make considered choices. They can publicly punish brands that don't meet their expectations and they can champion those that exceed their expectations.

For many consumers, this empowerment is a novelty that they're wielding with glee. For a younger generation coming into the market, it's all they've ever known. That means from here, there's only one way to go – forward.

What this means is that brands now need to find ways to 'attract' people. They need to become magnets for people and tribes.

Brands now need to find ways to 'attract' people. They need to become magnets for people and tribes.

For marketers, it means we have to think differently. We can no longer simply create the messages about our products that we want our audience to hear. We have to listen, really listen and understand what it is they want to know, what's important to them, what inspires them and why they'll invest their time listening to what we have to say.

3. The perennial Millennial quest for 'purpose'

The Millennial's desire to seek purpose in their lives is well documented. This desire is magnified even further for Gen Z, so businesses that want to be relevant to these generations moving forward are going to need to address what is fast becoming the fifth 'P' of marketing – 'purpose'.

As a generation, Millennials have a vision of a fairer, more inclusive, happier, thriving society. And if the traditional bastions of the corporate world won't move towards this vision, then they will go and create it themselves, as the growth in social enterprise globally reflects.

Deloitte's 2017 global Millennial survey highlights some interesting data on Millennial attitudes and expectations of business:

- 76 per cent of Millennials now regard business as a force for positive social impact.

- 88 per cent of Millennials say business, in general, around the world is having a positive impact on the wider society in which it operates, which reflects an optimistic view towards business.

When you look more closely though, an interesting qualifier to this data emerges:

- Only 59 per cent of survey respondents believe multi-national businesses have made a positive impact on the challenges that Millennials cited as their greatest concerns, e.g. economic and social progress, conflict, inequality, corruption, etc.

This figure is significantly below those who believe such organisations have the potential to make a positive impact (74 per cent). Overall, the impact gap stands at 15 points and is higher in mature markets (18 points) than in emerging markets (12 points).

This gap suggests that multinational businesses still have some way to go to address expectations of Millennials in society today.

Distrust of corporations, consumer empowerment and high expectations of Millennials are issues forcing businesses to consider their role in society.

Each one of these three issues alone is reason enough for businesses to reassess how they are contributing to society. The fact that all three of them are converging magnifies the need for businesses to consider what role they should play in society.

SYNCHRONICITY MEETS OPPORTUNITY

There's a lovely synchronicity around this whole subject of brand purpose, which has threaded its way through this chapter. So far, we have learned:

1. Society needs new ways to approach mounting problems.

2. People want business to do more to contribute positively to society. They have shown that they'll favour and support those businesses that step up.

3. Business needs to find new ways to market their brands. They need to attract people to their brands.

Purpose-led brands can change the world, attracting followers, supporters and collaborators along the way. Ultimately, a purpose-led approach builds strong, healthy and resilient brands. This is a win for society, a win for consumers and a win for business. That's the power of purpose for marketers today.

KEY POINTS

- Great brands sell much more than their product. They've managed to understand the reason they exist beyond money and beyond product.

- Not all brand purpose is related to causes or social responsibility. The power of brand purpose is in its value as a higher order mission – to inspire people to dream and imagine the extraordinary.

- Two fundamental checkpoints that a brand needs to deliver on for its brand purpose to be believable are credibility and authenticity.

- Purpose-led brands have immense focus and a long-term vision. Purpose provides a clear competitive edge against brands that focus on product differentiation.

- Three key issues forcing business to reassess its role in society and consider adopting a purpose-led strategy are as follows:

  1. Trust in corporations is rapidly declining.

  2. Technology disruption has created the age of the empowered consumer. Brands need to find ways to become magnets to people and tribes.

  3. Millennials have high expectations of business. Currently, there is a significant gap between what Millennials expect of multinational businesses and what they believe those businesses are delivering.

CHAPTER 2

DOING GOOD IS
GOOD FOR BUSINESS

Corporate social responsibility (CSR) was originally developed in response to an expectation of businesses to give back to society. The support of not-for-profit (NFP) partners was traditionally under the management of the corporate citizenship department. As much as it was seen as an obligation of the business, it was considered a *passive* part of the business – it didn't drive business growth and it wasn't expected to deliver a return. The choice of NFP partner often reflected this apathy; often being selected based on a personal connection. For example, the CEO's wife's favourite charity (apologies if this sounds sexist but that was indeed a reality for many companies a while back).

Over time, CSR has evolved to meet the growing need for employee engagement. NFP partners are now often selected based on the opportunity they deliver for volunteering. The corporate citizenship team look at how they can drive engagement between employees and the NFP partner to meet the increasing desire of employees to feel a sense of purpose where they work.

As this develops, CSR starts to take on a more active role within the business.

On another floor in the corporation's office, the marketing department are hard at work driving sales and market growth and building a brand that their target audience recognises and cares about. This is 100 per cent *active* work – it's all about delivering a return on investment to the business.

What is now starting to emerge is a model where the roles of CSR and marketing are more integrated, where corporate citizenship and brand marketing come together to build social and brand value. Businesses select causes to support that are strategically aligned with their brands and business objectives. Businesses consider how they can drive social impact, not just fundraising. They implement marketing strategies that leverage their partnerships and sometimes go further by offering their customers ways to get involved and also drive social impact. This is the essence of cause marketing.

Cause marketing has been around for many years, exemplified (not in the best way) about 10 or so years ago when Australia went 'pink' mad. Mount Franklin water launched a fundraising campaign in support of the National Breast Cancer Foundation and added a pink lid to every Mount Franklin water bottle. Within 18 months, Australians were faced with a tsunami of pink products across almost every category imaginable. Everything from biscuits to baked beans, newspapers to board games and sports shoes to our very own Sydney Opera House.

We can be a bit of a cynical bunch here in Australia and we can spot opportunism a mile away. In many of these 'pink partnerships' there was an absence of any authentic long-term commitment. Add to that the sometimes tenuous link between the brand and the cause and it would be reasonable to guess that many of those 'pink' cause campaigns didn't deliver what their marketing teams had hoped for. So, the pink noise died down and with it the initial stirrings of the cause marketing movement in Australia.

Fast-forward to today. Globally, consumers are telling businesses that they want more from them. Numerous research studies have consistent findings on this subject.

> *87 per cent of consumers believe that business needs to place at least equal weight on society's interests as on business interests.*[1]

Note the words '*at least* equal weight'. That is coming from almost 9 out of 10 people surveyed, heralding a major change in the public's expectation of business.

This expectation of brands hasn't just paved the way for for-profit brands to adopt cause and purpose-led marketing strategies, it has also led to the rise of social enterprise: for-profit businesses that trade to intentionally create positive social impact. We discussed the Thankyou organisation in Chapter 1 so here are some further examples of Australian social enterprises:

- *Who Gives A Crap.* A toilet 'roll model' that gives 50 per cent of its profits to WaterAid to build toilets in developing nations.

- *The Good Beer Co.* A company that brews Great Barrier Beer and donates 50 per cent of its profits to the Australian Marine Conservation Society.

According to a 2016 report Australia's social enterprise sector is thriving. Currently, there are at least 20,000 Australian social enterprises in operation and many of these are between two and five years old. The sector has seen a 37 per cent growth over the last five years and this growth is expected to continue.[2]

Against this backdrop, many established for-profit brands are struggling to remain relevant to their consumers.

Consider the following statistic:

> 'Most people wouldn't care if 74 per cent of brands disappeared in the future.'[3]

That's a significant figure, don't you think? Just consider it for a moment. Ask yourself the same question. Which brands would you really and truly care about if they disappeared? It's an interesting exercise and one that highlights the power and value of a brand that passes that test.

A few years ago, I lost a member of my team when I asked her this same question. Liz was one of our account managers. When she thought about the question, she decided there was one brand she really cared about and that was Qantas. A few months later, she approached me and announced her resignation. She was going to work for Qantas. She told me it hadn't previously crossed her mind to look for another job, but after doing that exercise, it really got her thinking. She said she really cared about Qantas and it made her realise that she would jump at the opportunity to work for them. She did a job search and, lo and behold, there was a job going in their marketing department.

That's got to tell you something. Caring about a brand has significant value. It attracts people to your brand – employees, partners and customers.

No doubt it's easier to build a brand that people care about when you have historic brand equity as the country's national airline carrier, or when you have millions of dollars to spend on advertising. For brands that don't fall into either of those categories, cause marketing can be another path to building a brand that people care about. A well-designed cause marketing program can give a brand strong social credentials, especially when it is leveraged consistently over a period of time.

93 per cent of consumers would buy a product associated with a cause.[4]

Welcome to cause marketing, folks!

People want brands to be socially and environmentally responsible. They are willing to try unknown brands with these credentials. For any brands that are socially and environmentally responsible, consumers are willing to pay more or even accept lower quality. According to Accenture's 'From Marketing to Mattering' study[5]:

- 80 per cent of people are willing to buy a product from an unknown brand with strong social and environmental credentials.

- 71 per cent of people say they are willing to pay more for a socially and environmentally responsible product.

- 57 per cent of people would purchase a product of lower efficacy or quality if it was more socially or environmentally responsible.

The Australian market follows the global trend favouring brands with social credentials. The 2012 Edelman goodpurpose® Study[6] findings show:

- 69 per cent of Australians think it's okay for brands to support good causes and make money at the same time.

- 68 per cent say they're more likely to purchase a product knowing that a portion of the money would go to a good cause.

- 58 per cent would switch brands if a different brand of similar quality supported a good cause.

Bear in mind that Australia hasn't been exposed to as much cause marketing as other markets so while these figures are impressive enough, we can only expect them to grow.

Edelman's research also highlights that people will advocate for purpose. They will recommend, promote and switch to brands that support good causes. Both the global and Australian study show high numbers in support of this.

Interestingly, the Edelman study also found that 71 per cent of people surveyed believe that brands and consumers could do more to support good causes by working together, and 63 per cent want brands to make it easier for them to make a positive difference.

That's a massive opportunity for brands.

Finally, if you're still not convinced then consider this – the bottom line.

In January 2017, Unilever released results from a new international study. The study asked 20,000 adults from five countries how their sustainability concerns impact their choices in-store and at home. Crucially, it then mapped their claims against real purchase decisions, giving a more accurate picture than ever of what people are actually buying – and why.

More than one in five (21 per cent) of the people surveyed said they would actively choose brands if they made their sustainability credentials clearer on their packaging and in their marketing.

The scale of this opportunity is further borne out by Unilever's own financial performance, as reported in the Unilever Sustainable Living Plan Summary of Progress 2016.[7] It highlights that Unilever's sustainable living brands (such as Dove, Ben & Jerry's and Continental, which have integrated sustainability into both their purpose and products) grew 50 per cent faster than the rest of the business and delivered over 60 per cent of the company's growth. Boom!

KEY POINTS

- Traditional CSR is evolving into a new model of cause marketing where corporate citizenship and brand marketing come together to build social *and* brand value.

- Australia's first period of cause marketing, beginning approximately 10 years ago, was largely opportunistic and will be mostly remembered as 'pink-washing'.

- Research highlights that consumers, globally and in Australia, expect businesses to contribute to society.

- This expectation has led to the growth of social enterprise organisations.

- Most people wouldn't care if 74 per cent of brands disappeared in the future.

- Research strongly reflects that consumers will favour brands that are aligned with a cause.

- Unilever brands that have integrated sustainability into both their purpose and products are collectively growing 50 per cent faster than the rest of the business.

---

1 Edelman, 2012, 'Edelman 2012 goodpurpose® Study', available at:
   http://www.edelman.com/insights/intellectual-property/good-purpose/
2 Finding Australia's Social Enterprise Sector (FASES) 2016 Report
   http://www.csi.edu.au/research/project/finding-australias-social-enterprise-sector-final-report-2016/
3 Havas Media Meaningful Brands Global Report http://www.meaningful-brands.com/en
4 2015 Cone Communications/Ebiquity Global CSR Opportunity Study
   http://www.conecomm.com/research-blog/2015-cone-communications-ebiquity-global-csr-study
5 Accenture Consulting, 'The Consumer Study: From Marketing to Mattering', available at:
   https://www.accenture.com/us-en/insight-un-global-compact-consumer-study-marketing-mattering
6 Edelman 2012 goodpurpose® Study Australia
   http://blog.edelman.com.au/2012/07/05/edelman-launches-goodpurpose-2012-with-australian-data/
7 https://www.unilever.com.au/Images/unilever-sustainable-living-plan-summary-of-progress-2016-anz_tcm1265-507753_1_en.pdf

CHAPTER 3

WHAT IS CAUSE MARKETING?

Over the last few years, as I have met with marketers on both the client and agency side, it has become apparent that there is a lot of confusion about what cause marketing is.

I frequently give presentations to provide clarity on this subject and include insights, research and some incredible case studies. I can't tell you the number of times I have given a group presentation and had the following experience. You've probably been in this situation yourself – either as a presenter or as an audience member. The audience file into a meeting room, most not knowing exactly what they're here to see. At this stage, they often look a bit fed up. Let's face it, they're probably under insane time pressures on a project and losing an hour for yet another meeting or presentation is not a welcome prospect. Their body language is negative, they're closed off and the vibe in the room generally feels like they just want to get this over and done with.

I should say, not all my meetings start this way but you can understand why many do. I understand only too well the pressure of deadlines, the monotony of a boring presentation and the frustration of time-wasting meetings. But I've done this presentation enough times to know that it has never been received negatively and rarely neutrally – quite the opposite, in fact.

As I take the audience through the presentation, the vibe in the room shifts quickly.

The interest in the subject is palpable. The audience's body language changes visibly and people start asking questions and contributing their thoughts. I love that moment, that shift. For me, that is the moment that you see the spark of possibility – the excitement in the value that these people want to bring to the world as they recognise how that value can be a reality. It's within their reach. And that response is not limited to Millennial marketers. It's a similar response from marketers of all generations.

I like to think it comes down to a simple human truth. We all want to contribute positively to this world of ours. We just need to be shown a way that we can do it easily.

Cause marketing is defined as the alignment of a for-profit brand with a cause to unlock social and brand value. It should not be confused with CSR or a company's efforts to be a good citizen. Cause marketers are unapologetic about working to extract commercial value from a cause marketing program – just as much as they are focused on creating positive social impact for the cause they support.

CSR is an organisation's commitment to contribute responsibly to society. It can encompass a range of things from sustainability efforts and ethical behaviours to support for non-profit partners.

Historically, non-profit partners were often selected subjectively according to relationships with or causes supported by the CEO or their spouse or other senior executives. More recently, recognition of the value of CSR to a business's wider efforts has seen more emphasis placed on a strategic alignment between a business and the cause partner it chooses to support.

Cause marketing can be a part of a business's CSR efforts, but it can also stand quite separately to CSR. An example of this is Caltex's Star Mart Wish Drive in partnership with Make-A-Wish Australia, which is discussed in detail in Chapter 16.

Make-A-Wish Australia was not an existing corporate partner to Caltex prior to the launch of the Star Mart Wish Drive campaign.

Caltex's retail marketing team had a strong desire to recapture some of the community goodwill they developed many years previously through their partnership with Starlight Children's Foundation.

This, combined with a motivation to contribute to a worthy cause, drove the campaign. Today, Make-A-Wish Australia is featured as one of the non-profit partners supported by Caltex through their corporate partnerships. So, in this case, a cause marketing effort drove adoption of a corporate partnership.

Cause marketing can therefore be a part of a business's CSR or citizenship efforts. I believe where it has its most valuable impact is when CSR and marketing come together to unlock both brand and social value. That is what we're seeing more and more today.

Then there is purpose-led marketing. Again, there is a big difference between this and cause marketing, although cause marketing can be a great way of bringing a brand's purpose to life.

Cause marketing tends to be campaign focused – it is a 'push', a drive, a campaign, an effort. Purpose-led marketing, on the other hand, is embedded in the DNA of a brand. It is what a brand stands for and fights for. The brand has a vision – a strategically aligned, socially-grounded brand purpose – that it moves closer to every day. The brand essentially becomes an activist for its purpose. Often the brand's stakeholders – its employees, customers and partners – become what I like to call 'brand citizens' who also support that purpose. If the way the company does business is at odds with its purpose, a true purpose-led brand will inevitably change the way it does business, even at the cost of profit.

EXAMPLES OF PURPOSE-LED BRANDS

For me, Patagonia stands out as one of the very best examples of a true purpose-led brand. You can read more about Patagonia and what defines it as a purpose-led brand in Chapter 8.

As I noted in the introduction, Procter & Gamble (P&G) has long had purpose-led marketing strategies for its brands, most notably for its nappy brand Pampers. Pampers is all about caring for babies' happy and healthy development. The brand's goal to eliminate Maternal and Neonatal Tetanus (MNT) in partnership with UNICEF is a cause marketing program that single-mindedly supports the brand's purpose. You can read more about this amazing program in Chapter 6.

Here at home, we have Zambrero. Zambrero is a healthy, quick-service Mexican restaurant whose tagline is 'Mexican with a mission'. Zambrero is also a humanitarian enterprise committed to tackling world hunger through its Plate 4 Plate initiative. Chapter 18 highlights the inspiring Zambrero story.

For marketers who want to get their brand on the path to purpose and don't know how to start, cause marketing can be a very effective way to begin this journey.

Regardless of whether you want to build a purpose-led brand or you just want your brand to be active in cause marketing, authenticity is an essential foundation to both of these approaches. It's vitally important to be authentic when choosing a cause or cause partner that is strategically aligned with your brand, as well as being authentic in your motivation to create social impact.

KEY POINTS

- Cause marketing is defined as the alignment of a for-profit brand with a cause to unlock social and brand value.

- Cause marketers are unapologetic about working to extract commercial value from a cause marketing program just as much as they are focused on creating positive social impact for the cause they support.

- Cause marketing can be a part of a company's CSR efforts or it can be a standalone marketing initiative.

- Cause marketing tends to be campaign-focused whereas purpose-led marketing is embedded into the DNA of a brand.

- Cause marketing can be a part of a purpose-led brand approach.

- Authenticity is an essential foundation to a cause marketing campaign and to building a purpose-led brand.

CHAPTER 4

THE SCIENCE BEHIND CAUSE MARKETING

Smile and the world smiles with you

Have you ever watched someone eating a piece of chocolate while you're not? Did it make you feel good? According to scientists, we have something in our brain called mirror neurons. They 'mirror' what you're watching, which means when you watch your friend eating that chocolate bar, your mirror neurons light up so that you feel some of the same endorphin hit that the chocolate eater experiences without eating any yourself. How good is that? It's connected with our motor and cognitive functions of empathy.

If you're not convinced about this, try standing up in front of a group of people and yawning. You'll soon discover that it's contagious!

Apart from giving you a great diet tactic or making you yawn, I tell you this little fact because it raises the very interesting subject of emotional triggers in marketing.

Think about this for a moment. Every single thing we desire comes down to a feeling we're chasing. You want that promotion at work? That's probably because you want to feel successful or rewarded for your efforts. You want to buy a new car? You may want to feel independent, but if it's a status brand, again, it may be that you want to feel successful. You want to travel the world? That could be a feeling of freedom or vitality that you're after. You want to get married? You probably want to feel loved or maybe you're after the 'happily ever after' feeling of security.

The list goes on.

If you want to take up a new hobby, perhaps you want to feel challenged or creative. Or if you want to do a parachute jump, it's most likely because you want to feel the adrenalin pumping through your body as you conquer your fear.

So, when it comes to marketing, we marketers are all trying to instil some kind of feeling in the audience that we're targeting. That's even true when we're communicating a discount offer or a cash-back because, in that instance, we are offering shoppers a chance to feel something. Think about how you feel when you've snapped up a bargain – smart, savvy, maybe even a little smug?

The thing about mirror neurons is that it means we are all hard-wired for empathy. Replace the image in your mind of someone eating a chocolate with the following images:

Imagine a puppy who has been abused, who looks beaten and uncared for and has the look of fear but also hope on its face. How does that make you feel?

Imagine a hungry child looking at you through the lens of the camera or a woman with her children who is a victim of domestic violence, who has to sleep out on the street or in her car. She probably had a normal, happy existence at one point in her life.

I'm not suggesting that you should be leveraging images like these for cause marketing. Let's see however what happens when we reverse the psychology.

Visualise the happy, energetic and fabulous celebration of Sydney's Gay and Lesbian Mardi Gras. How does that make you feel when you imagine that? (I'll share with you later in the book the amazing case study of ANZ and their 11-year support of Sydney's Gay and Lesbian Mardi Gras.)

Or imagine in your mind's eye the look of happiness and delight from a child who you've helped to feed, clothe or educate.

These are all incredibly powerful feelings, both the negative and the positive.

What cause marketing offers its audience can be summed up in one word: happiness.

If I can contribute something to help alleviate someone's pain or unhappiness, I feel like I've done something worthwhile. It makes me feel happy. As a marketer, that's the most powerful feeling that you can incite, except perhaps love but I would argue that realistically, love is beyond most marketers' remit, whereas happiness is attainable by most.

There's a lot of research around the science of happiness and what people can do to increase their happiness. One of the most consistently documented contributors to happiness is 'giving'. Numerous studies show that giving back or being kind makes us feel less stressed, more connected, open to new experiences and happier.

In one famous study, students were asked to commit five random acts of kindness each week over a six-week period. Those who did showed a 42 per cent increase in their happiness, whereas the group who didn't experienced a reduction in wellbeing.[1] Another study, conducted in 2006, found that simply reflecting on nice things we've done for other people can lift our mood.[2]

What this means is that cause marketers are in the happiness business. What's more, as cause marketers, we not only get to deliver campaigns that contribute to people feeling happy, we also get to feel a sense of real fulfilment in the work we're doing.

That's been borne out by my own experiences. The teams I've worked with on cause marketing campaigns have felt inspired, energised and fulfilled in their work. The teams looking on have felt happy for their colleagues but perhaps a little jealous that they weren't involved themselves. The marketers involved in the case studies mentioned in this book speak about those campaigns with such pride.

What this means is that cause marketers are in the happiness business.

There is no doubt that cause marketing has numerous benefits for the target audience, the cause, the brand and for the team involved in bringing a cause marketing program to life. What is reassuring is to understand that the appeal of cause marketing is not simply part of an ephemeral trend – it's linked to the fundamental human capacity for empathy. While levels of empathy may differ in individuals, we can be utterly confident that empathy is an enduring human neurophysiological function that is not going to disappear anytime soon.

KEY POINTS

- Mirror neurons in our brain mean we are hardwired for empathy.

- Cause marketing is all about tapping into people's capacity for empathy.

- What cause marketing offers its audience can be summed up in one word: happiness.

- One of the most consistently documented contributors to happiness is 'giving'.

- Cause marketers are in the happiness business – not only do they get to deliver campaigns that make people feel happy, they also feel more fulfilled themselves.

- Cause marketing is not simply part of an ephemeral trend – it's linked to the fundamental human capacity for empathy.

---

1   Interventions to boost happiness and buttress resilience http://sonjalyubomirsky.com/wp-content/themes/sonjalyubomirsky/papers/LDinpressb.pdf
2   University of Southampton 2006 Study 'Nostalgia: Content, Triggers, Functions' http://www.wildschut.me/Tim_Wildschut/home_files/Nostalgia%20JPSP.pdf

CHAPTER 5

12 WAYS TO APPROACH CAUSE MARKETING

People often ask me about the different ways cause marketing can be approached. In this chapter, I highlight some of the most commonly used approaches, provide examples of how they can be used and discuss the benefits to the parties involved.

It's worth noting that many campaigns use a combination of these approaches to leverage their partnership and achieve their social and business goals. This allows for a richer, deeper experience for the customer while also increasing the chances of success for the brand's drive for social impact and business growth.

1. SPONSORSHIP/LICENSING/CO-BRANDING

This is where a brand sponsors or licenses a NFP brand (or the NFP's existing campaign) and leverages it via marketing. It's no different to the way a brand might approach sponsoring a sporting event or team.

Example: Cricket Australia's Pink Test in partnership with the McGrath Foundation.

The Pink Test, also known as Jane McGrath Day, is held each year in January at the Sydney Cricket Ground on day three of Cricket Australia's test match. It is held in honour of Glenn McGrath's late wife who died of breast cancer in 2008. Everyone is invited to wear pink and fundraise to help meet an overall target amount. In 2017, the target was $390,000. Over $500,000 was raised.

Benefits to the promoter – Cricket Australia:
- Builds goodwill – creates awareness of Cricket Australia's 'Cricket Cares' program and builds the organisation's credentials as a good corporate citizen and community contributor.
- Promotes Cricket Australia as an authentic and trustworthy organisation, given the strong ties between the cricket community, Glenn and Jane McGrath and the McGrath Foundation. The commitment of Cricket Australia to this cause is also an authenticity driver as 2017 marks the Pink Test's ninth year.
- Increases support for Cricket Australia while also creating 'news' and a high point of the calendar, driving more spectators and ticket sales.
- Deepens engagement with existing fans.
- Promotes the game to women and families and increases its appeal to these target audiences.

Benefits to the NFP partner – McGrath Foundation:
- Builds the profile and drives awareness of the Foundation and its important work in the community.
- Allows for a huge fundraising opportunity.

Benefits to customers – Cricket fans:
- Enables them to express their support by wearing pink on the day and donating to a good cause.
- Makes them feel good while enjoying a fun day out in support of a good cause.

2. TRANSACTIONAL (PORTION OF PROCEEDS)

This is a commonly used approach where a brand pledges a percentage or dollar or cent amount from its proceeds to be donated to the cause. Usually a minimum donation amount will be agreed between the brand and the NFP partner. The brand's business is obliged to pay this minimum amount regardless of sales. This gives the NFP partner some protection in the event sales do not deliver as expected. It's very reasonable for the NFP partner to demand a minimum donation, given the brand partner is leveraging the brand equity and emotional equity in the NFP partner's brand.

Example: Bakers Delight Pink Bun campaign in support of Breast Cancer Network Australia (BCNA).

Since 2000, Bakers Delight has raised more than $3.7 million for BCNA, directly supporting thousands of Australian women and their families through their breast cancer journey. The Bakers Delight Pink Bun campaign runs annually across all Bakers Delight bakeries across Australia. During the campaign period (which lasts for approximately three weeks), 100 per cent of sales of pink finger buns and BCNA Pink Ladies are donated to BCNA to fund 'My Journey Kits' that are distributed to women who are newly diagnosed with breast cancer.

Benefits to the promoter – Bakers Delight:

- Positions Bakers Delight as a brand that gives back and contributes to the community which, in turn, builds brand health.
- Generates sales by creating news and giving people a reason to come to Bakers Delight.
- Generates incremental sales of other Bakers Delight products.
- Instils a sense of purpose among Bakers Delight franchisees and employees.

Benefits to NFP partner – BCNA:
- Generates funding through donations
- Increases awareness for the foundation.

Benefits to Bakers Delight customers:
- Enables them to express their support by buying a pink bun and donating to a good cause.

3. FUNDRAISING

This is when brands and for-profit organisations fundraise for their NFP partner organisations using their brand assets to invite their customers to donate.

Cricket Australia's Pink Test is a great example of combined sponsorship/co-branding and fundraising. The Caltex Star Mart Wish Drive combined a number of fundraising techniques to raise money and awareness for Make-A-Wish Australia.

Example: Caltex Star Mart Wish Drive for Make-A-Wish Australia.

Since 2013, Caltex has supported Make-A-Wish Australia by raising funds through the Star Mart Wish Drive. The 2013 and 2014 campaigns involved local store marketing, in-store barbecues, gala days and driveway service days to fundraise across 300+ stores. Some of Caltex's suppliers also donated a percentage of sales on marked products to Make-A-Wish.

Benefits to the promoter – Caltex:
- Builds awareness of the local site and attracts new customers.
- Positions the brand and the local business as one that cares about community issues which, in turn, builds more trust in the brand.
- Drives incremental sales across other fundraising products being sold by Caltex.

Benefits to the NFP partner – Make-A-Wish Australia:
- Generates funding through donations
- Increases awareness for Make-A-Wish.

Benefits to Caltex customers:
- Enables them to express their support by donating and/or buying participating marked products.

4. AWARENESS-DRIVING

Awareness-driving is when a brand uses its assets to drive awareness of a cause partner's offering to their customer base. This approach is often, but not always, combined with either fundraising or a transactional proceeds mechanic.

Example: UberPUPPIES.

In 2016, Uber teamed up with Purina's Pets at Work mission to bring UberPUPPIES to eight cities in Australia via local animal shelter organisations in each city. In a single day event, Uber customers were invited to open their app between 12pm and 4pm and request the 'PUPPIES' option. If puppies were available, an Uber driver would bring one to your workplace for 15 minutes of puppy love. People paid a $40 snuggle fee and Uber and Purina in turn supported the participating animal shelters. Plus, every puppy snuggler also received an Uber and Purina gift bag. All puppies were also up for adoption.

Benefits to the promoter – Uber:
- Promotes Uber as a brand that cares and has goodwill.
- Massive positive public relations and awareness boost.
- Increased customer reach as non-Uber customers had to download the app if they wanted to participate.

Benefits to the NFP partner – Purina Pets at Work mission and local animal shelters:

- Raises awareness for NFP organisations.
- Drives more adoptions for pets in shelters.

Benefits to customers:

- Well, if you got to snuggle a puppy then your benefit was plenty of endorphins and oxytocin! For those of us (and there were many) who missed out – a lot of disappointment but, speaking from personal experience, this didn't seem to reflect negatively on Uber at all.

5. PRODUCT DONATION

Brands sometimes provide in-kind support to organisations. While NFPs generally prefer monetary donations, sometimes products can be a valuable resource for them.

Example: The Dulux Surf Club Project.

Since 2011, Dulux has been a partner of Surf Life Saving Australia. The Dulux Surf Club Project provides all surf clubs in Australia with 100 litres of free Weathershield paint every year, for the duration of the program, to paint the interior and exterior of their surf clubs (more on this great initiative in Chapter 12).

Benefit to the promoter – Dulux:

- Reinforces the key benefit of the Weathershield product – protection against the elements.
- Positions the brand as an active contributor to local communities.

Benefit to the NFP partner – Surf Life Saving Australia:

- Saves each club costs that they would otherwise spend on paint.

- Drives awareness of the organisation.
- Generates funding via sponsorship fees.

Benefit to customers:

- When they buy Dulux, they know they are buying a brand that supports an iconic Australian organisation at a grassroots level.

6. MATCH DONATIONS

This is when a brand will invite their customers to make a donation to its nominated charity partner. The brand pledges to match every donation made as a result of the campaign.

Example: Patagonia's The Double Down campaign.

Hosted on Pozible, The Double Down is Patagonia Australia's matched donation campaign that saw crowdfunded donations to six grassroots environmental groups matched dollar-for-dollar by Patagonia up to a combined total of $100,000.

Benefit to the promoter – Patagonia:

- Delivers on their brand mission statement, 'To build the best product, cause no unnecessary harm, use business to inspire and implement solutions to the environmental crisis.'
- Promotes awareness of and engagement with their brand to a new audience via the Pozible platform.
- Inspires collaboration with their customers and supporters, deepening the relationship between brand and consumer.

Benefit to the NFP partners – various grassroots community projects:

- Increases awareness of their causes.
- Generates fundraising for several community projects.

Benefit to customers:
- Educates them across a diverse range of environmental issues and projects.
- Offers them choice and makes it easy for them to contribute to a project of their choice.

7. ACTION FACILITATION

This is an approach where a brand makes it easy for people to contribute to a good cause.

Example: Optus RockCorps.

Optus RockCorps invites Australians to volunteer four hours of their time on community projects and, in return, they get access to an exclusive concert that is for volunteers only.

Benefit to the promoter – Optus:
- Promotes engagement with their brand to a young audience.
- Positions the brand as a community contributor.

Benefit to the NFP partner – various grassroots community projects:
- Generates a boost in volunteers for their projects.

Benefit to customers:
- Makes it easy for them to contribute to their communities by trading their time rather than needing to donate money.
- Rewards the volunteers and makes them feel significant.

8. CHARITY STICKER PROMOTIONS OR PIN-UP CAMPAIGNS

This approach is used mostly by retailers. Retailers invite their customers to buy a charity sticker and then it is displayed on the retailer's wall. The money paid for the sticker goes to the NFP partner organisation.

Example: Coles is giving Redkite a helping hand.

Coles and Redkite have been partnering since 2013. One of their many fundraising activities invites shoppers to pay $2 for a Redkite sticker which is then displayed on a wall in Coles to show their support.

Benefit to the promoter – Coles:
- Generates goodwill towards the Coles brand.
- Promotes brand engagement between Coles and its customers.

Benefit to the NFP partner – Redkite:
- Allows for an increase in fundraising.
- Drives awareness of the Redkite brand.

Benefit to customers:
- Makes it easy for them to contribute to a cause.
- Makes them feel good about themselves for donating to the cause and they can see a token of their donation every time they are in store.

9. ONE-FOR-ONE

This is a transactional model where a brand donates one of 'something' to a cause or NFP partner for every sale of a certain product.

Example: Zambrero Plate 4 Plate.

Plate 4 Plate is Zambrero's way of tackling world hunger. For every burrito or bowl purchased at Zambrero, a meal is donated to someone in need.

Benefits to the promoter – Zambrero:
- Provides a unique and marketable point of difference in the market.

- Drives strong appeal for the brand.
- Attracts and retains employees who become invested in the brand's work.

Benefits to the NFP partner – Stop Hunger Now:
- Increases awareness for the cause
- Generates fundraising for their cause.

Benefits to customers:
- Makes them feel good about their purchase because they're contributing positively to another person's life.

10. BRAND ACTIVISM

This is when brands take a stand for something. Brand activism is such a powerful opportunity for brands, but it can also be risky. This approach is likely to create brand fans but also some detractors, who may not support what the brand stands for.

Example: Ben & Jerry's Fight for the Reef Scoop Tour.

In 2014, in response to the Great Barrier Reef (GBF) Marine Park Authority approving a plan to expand a coal port and dump three million cubic metres of dredge spoil in the GBR marine park, Ben & Jerry's launched its Fight for the Reef Scoop Tour in partnership with the World Wildlife Fund (WWF) Australia. Their goal was to give out free Ben & Jerry's, raise awareness about the dangers facing the GBR and encourage Australians to join the fight to save their landmark.

Benefits to the promoter – Ben & Jerry's:
- Provides a unique and marketable point of difference for the brand.
- Creates passionate fans of the brand.
- Shows that the brand is socially responsible and cares about environmental issues.

Benefits to the NFP partner – WWF:
- Raises awareness of the issues facing the GBF and Australia's environment.
- Builds support for their cause.

Benefits to customers:
- Educates and enables them to do something positive for Australia while also receiving free ice cream!

11. PURPOSE-DRIVING

A purpose-driven brand stands for something and consistently supports that cause through everything it does. It is a brand that stands for something more than profit.

Example: Dove Real Beauty.

In a world of stereotypes, Dove recognises that beauty comes in all shapes and sizes.

Benefit to the promoter – Dove:
- A long-term positioning that provides an authentic, unique and marketable point of difference in a category that is dominated by stereotypical images of beauty.
- Emotionally engages their consumers by championing the fight against media stereotypes

Benefit to the cause:
- A strong voice against the stereotypes women continue to be pressured to conform to.

Benefit to customers:
- Empowering women to celebrate their own unique beauty.
- Inspiring women and girls to build body confidence and self-esteem.

12. MERCHANDISE FOR SALE

This is one of the oldest ways that charities and NFP partners generate fundraising – by providing branded merchandise to retail partners for sale to their customers at the point of purchase. An example of this is something like Daffodil Day pens which you might buy at a retailer.

Benefits to the promoter:
- There are few benefits for the promoter using this approach. The association between the promoter and the cause or NFP partner is disconnected at best. However, if the promoter can offer a piece of merchandise that is exclusive and unique to its brand then there is opportunity for the merchandise to be more accurately associated to the brand. Depending on what the merchandise is, and how much value the shopper attributes to it, there could be some corresponding value.

Benefits to the NFP partner:
- Allows for fundraising at a time when the shopper is already spending money.
- Raises awareness of the cause.

Benefits to customers:
- Satisfaction at being able to easily support a cause.

KEY POINTS

- There is a whole range of ways to approach cause marketing.

- The 12 approaches documented in this chapter are simply a starting point to give you some inspiration.

PART 2

INSPIRATION: BRANDS THAT ARE CHANGING THE WORLD

CHAPTER 6

PAMPERS AND UNICEF

One pack = one vaccine

In May 2012, I visited Chicago to attend the Cause Marketing Forum Conference, now known as the Engage for Good Conference. It was an eye-opening experience for me. The sheer scale and sophistication of cause marketing outside of Australia hit me like a high-speed train.

Each year at the conference, one company and one NFP is recognised for overall excellence. In 2012, the company recognised was Procter & Gamble (P&G), a cause marketing pioneer for more than three decades that has successfully implemented purpose-led marketing strategies for most of its brands.

Its campaigns include:

- *Tide Loads of Hope.* Tide is a laundry detergent brand that sent a mobile laundromat to disaster stricken areas to wash, dry and fold clothing for free.
- *Dawn's Everyday Wildlife Champions.* Dawn is a dish-washing detergent that donates product and funds to help clean wildlife that has been affected by oil spills.

- *Pampers one pack = one vaccine.* This initiative aims to protect women and their babies against Maternal and Neonatal Tetanus (MNT).

The following case study for Pampers one pack = one vaccine is a study in cause marketing excellence. Beyond being a gold standard though, I believe it offers marketers inspiration for how they can use their chosen careers in a meaningful and impactful way by building a strong brand that stands for something, uniting their colleagues in action and creating meaningful social impact.

CASE STUDY: PAMPERS ONE PACK = ONE VACCINE

Background

In 2004, the disposable nappy market in Europe and North America was dominated by two strong brands, Pampers and Huggies. Competition on product features was fierce but, for consumers, the nappy category was low interest. Purchasers often made their brand choice depending on price. Category sales were flat and the struggle for market share was intense. Pampers led the global market with particularly strong performance results in Europe. However, Huggies led the market in North America. With worldwide sales at US$9 billion, Pampers was P&G's leading brand. Therefore, the need to build brand loyalty in order to maintain its leadership position was a priority.

Against this background, the P&G team recognised that while it was important to maintain competitiveness in product attributes, the bigger opportunity was to develop an emotional connection to the Pampers brand. Their challenge, following current best practice in branding, was to promote Pampers' core essence as the brand that cares for babies' happy and healthy development.

Testing

The original campaign was tested in Belgium in 2004. It was launched as a Christmas campaign and was called Silent Night. It was built around a sleeping baby commercial, UNICEF's Christmas card campaign and children's vaccinations. The television commercial (TVC) promised parents a 'good night's sleep' and invited them to work together with Pampers and UNICEF to help all babies all over the world to sleep in peace.

The original proposition was complex. Shoppers who bought a Pampers jumbo pack of nappies received three UNICEF Christmas cards. For each of these purchases, Pampers promised to donate the cost of eight polio vaccines to UNICEF. In addition, UNICEF inserted donation solicitations in Pampers' direct mail packs, allowing parents to separately donate to the campaign if they wanted to.

The promotion ran for five weeks from mid-November, ending just before Christmas. Despite only being supported by one major store chain, the campaign got a lot of media attention and results showed that Pampers' volume share for December 2004 had indexed 103 compared with the previous year. That was considered a good result in a period that was traditionally slow for the category, particularly given the limited time of the campaign and the limited retail support.

The social results in that first year were also good. The proceeds from the donations funded the immunisation of 200,000 children against polio.

The following year, the campaign was simplified. The vaccination program against polio remained the supported cause. The promotion still focused on the Pampers jumbo pack of nappies. This time though, no Christmas cards were included and the messaging promised to 'vaccinate one child with the purchase of one pack of nappies'. Once again, UNICEF was able to insert their fundraising literature into Pampers' direct mail packs.

This time, national trade partners responded positively with in-store displays and out-of-store support in the form of retailer mailings to customers that included Pampers' promotion details.

Once more, Pampers' volume share increased by another 3 per cent over the previous year and, once again, donations to UNICEF were significant.

At that stage, P&G recognised that it had a campaign idea that had merit and could potentially expand, but P&G wanted to build something more strategic. Both P&G and UNICEF wanted to continue to activate the campaign during Christmas, given it's a time of year when people are in a giving mindset but also because of the lack of trade interest in the nappy category at that time of year.

Beyond that, however, P&G wanted to refine the concept so that the campaign was clearer, simpler, and more compelling – and it would play to the two brands' core essence, not just be a seasonal promotion.

Eventually, after running some research focus groups in the UK with hardcore private label customers, P&G identified the sheer emotional power of the concept of a single vaccine donation with each pack of nappies purchased. Its mechanic – one pack = one vaccine – was locked in.

Identifying the Maternal and Neonatal Tetanus (MNT) program

Now P&G needed to find a vaccination program through UNICEF that was affordable to support a single pack purchase mechanic. When UNICEF came back with a list of vaccine programs, the MNT program stood out – not just from a cost perspective but also because it aligned with Pampers' brand positioning, caring for babies' happy and healthy development.

In 2006, MNT affected people in some of the poorest and most remote areas in the world. It is essentially caused by exposure to unhygienic conditions during childbirth. For example, when a kitchen knife is used to cut an umbilical cord, resulting in the baby and/or mother contracting tetanus. The disease is fatal for about 70 per cent of infants who contract it and it was estimated that about 30,000 mothers were dying annually as a result of contracting MNT.

At the time of the inception of the Pampers and UNICEF partnership, the World Health Organization (WHO) estimated that someone was dying every four minutes from this very preventable disease. This was the program P&G and UNICEF decided to support through their cause marketing partnership.

European campaign roll-out

Christmas 2006 saw the launch of the one pack = one vaccine program that continues today. Initially, the campaign ran in the UK, Ireland, the Netherlands and Belgium and included specially marked packs of the Pampers baby range, rather than just the jumbo pack of nappies.

Trade partners supported the campaign enthusiastically. Media coverage was exceptional across all markets. The results below will give you a sense of the success of the campaign:

United Kingdom:
- 3 per cent volume share increase for October/November/December period compared with the previous quarter.
- Volume share versus the same period of the previous year remained consistent.
- Strong improvement on image perception across all key brand attributes compared to the previous period.

Netherlands:

- 4 per cent volume share increase compared with the previous year.

From a social impact perspective, the donations generated for UNICEF by this campaign were substantial. Although, it was decided to drop the inserts of solicitation material into Pampers' direct mail packs as the impact of this part of the program was less successful.

During the following year's Christmas period, the program rolled out to cover 16 countries in Western Europe. The market response was enthusiastic. Retailers were eager to get onboard with some retailers mounting their own supplementary efforts such as adopting a specific country to support towards eliminating the disease.

Celebrities also got involved, which increased the profile of this initiative even further. Celebrities such as Salma Hayek and Emma Bunton have enabled the program to continually achieve consumer interest and support.

Global roll-out and impact

By the end of the 2007 campaign, P&G and UNICEF deepened their commitment to the program by deciding to roll the campaign out globally and setting a goal to work together to eliminate MNT from the world.

This, for me, is a defining moment – a brand making a commitment to a global social goal. I don't think I've ever heard of anything quite like this before or since. Don't forget that this is a marketing campaign – a campaign which started as a way to drive commercial sales and build brand equity.

Through this initiative, Pampers evolved from being a brand that promised dry bottoms and a good night's sleep to a brand that stood for happy, healthy babies around the world, working with its trade partners, its customers and UNICEF to deliver this.

It has now been more than 10 years since the 2006 launch of this campaign. The social results are absolutely mind-blowing:

- 500,000 newborn babies have been saved
- 300 million vaccines have been administered
- The campaign has helped eliminate MNT in 17 countries.

This goes way beyond showcasing a powerful cause marketing program. This Pampers initiative offers up a shining example of how a brand can stand for something – credibly and authentically. In doing so, Pampers has become an educator and an activist.

When I attended the keynote presentation from Nada Dugas, Communications Director of P&G, at the cause marketing conference, it was clear that she was someone who had been very close to this program over the years.

There was one moment during Nada's presentation when she talked about the longevity of the program. She said that one of the biggest challenges was keeping the business focused on the program and that new marketers often came in wanting to do something new and different. Her response was visceral. She said that the Pampers and UNICEF campaign was one of P&G's most successful marketing campaigns globally and P&G would continue to run this program until they had successfully eliminated MNT globally.

My take-out from Nada's presentation was that she was emotionally invested in this program. I believe, as a marketer, she had full permission to be so invested given the program had delivered compelling marketing and sales results.

This, for me, is a defining moment – a brand making a commitment to a global social goal.

This is what brand power looks like when it's used for good. Amazing, isn't it?

Note: Alongside the consumer-facing campaign, P&G also activated the program internally. It is the most over-subscribed internal engagement program that I have heard of. I write about this more in Chapter 21 – Internal alignment and engagement.

SIX KEY TAKE-OUTS FROM PAMPERS' APPROACH TO CAUSE MARKETING

1. *Cause marketing can trump lowest price.* Pampers still had to be competitive on product features, but the campaign enabled the brand to emotionally connect with its consumers and gave them a compelling reason, beyond price, to choose Pampers nappies over competing products.

2. *Relevance drives credibility.* The alignment between Pampers' brand positioning – Pampers cares for babies' happy, healthy development – and the UNICEF program to target and eradicate MNT was foundational in driving the credibility and success of the program.

3. *Defining a social impact goal builds authenticity and provides a powerful platform to engage stakeholders.* Pampers' goal to eliminate MNT from the globe was huge and positioned the brand as an activist, attracting consumers, employees and celebrity ambassadors.

4. *Trade partners can be enthusiastic supporters of a cause program.* This campaign highlighted the power of a strategically led cause marketing program to rally retailers to support and amplify the program.

5. *Longevity enables genuine impact and strategic storytelling.* A brand that's bold enough to try to eradicate a disease from the world creates a powerful storytelling

platform and elevates itself in the hearts and minds of consumers.

6. *Internal engagement of a cause marketing program has benefits outside of marketing.* Pampers' business unit now posts among the company's highest rates of employee satisfaction due, in large part, to the internal engagement program linked to this program (see Chapter 21 for more on this).

CHAPTER 7

SHAKE SHACK

The Great American Shake Sale

Shake Shack is an American quick-service restaurant (QSR) that serves hot dogs, hamburgers and milkshakes. Since its establishment in 2004 it has become one of the fastest growing food chains and is now a public company. As of 2016, Shake Shack had 100 locations across the US.

If you visit the Shake Shack website, you'll see that the brand places an emphasis on standing for something good. That includes the ingredients it sources and the deep community support it is actively involved in through donations, events and volunteering.

One of the programs that Shake Shack has invested in since 2012 is a cause marketing program called The Great American Shake Sale. Shake Shack partners with NFP organisation Share Our Strength for this campaign, working with their No Kid Hungry program to raise money towards the goal to end childhood hunger in the US.

The program takes its name from one of Share Our Strength's existing programs called The Great American Bake Sale. Through this program, people are invited to host bake sales in their communities to fundraise for the No Kid Hungry program.

Every year, throughout the month of May, Shake Shack customers are invited to donate a minimum of $2 and, in return, they receive a voucher for a free shake, valued at $5, to use on their next visit to Shake Shack. One hundred per cent of the donations received go to the No Kid Hungry program.

To reinforce the campaign's link with The Great American Bake Sale, Shake Shack created seven bake-sale-inspired custard shake flavours to be featured in their May Custard Calendar, including flavours such as oatmeal crème pie, chocolate chip cookie and banana bread.

The campaign was communicated in-store, online and via social media. Plus, all Shake Shack staff wore No Kid Hungry branded uniforms during the campaign period.

At the heart of this campaign was an incredibly strong internal staff engagement program. Share our Strength provided resources to help train Shake Shack staff which included fact sheets and employee training videos that highlighted real stories of hunger. It enabled Shake Shack staff to be able to educate guests clearly about what the campaign was and the change they wanted to create. Localised fact sheets created by Share Our Strength summarised the state of hunger in the location's state. These fact sheets were shared with guests waiting in line to order and were printed on the back of the May Custard Calendars. This ensured that by the time guests reached the counter to order, they were well prepared for the $2 donation request.

To date, through the US campaign, Shake Shack customers have donated close to $2 million. Here is a breakdown of the funds raised since the launch of the program:

- 2012 = $136,000
- 2013 = $285,000 (+110 per cent)

- 2014 = $338, 000 (+18 per cent)
- 2015 = $504,000 (+49 per cent)
- 2016 = $597,000 (+18 per cent)

As you can see from their fundraising results, each year participation levels for the campaign have grown. This will partially be because of the growth of the business and the increase in the number of Shake Shack locations. However, it's reasonable to believe that the growth is also due to an increase in awareness of the program.

I've had a lot of experience over the years in leveraging sponsorships for brands. For sponsorships that are integrated with sporting franchises, where there is an annual activation, it is common to see participation levels grow. In fact, as awareness grows, the need for media to drive awareness around the event reduces. This means that brands can afford to spend less if they wish and still get the same or better sales increase and participation levels.

The same principle works for annual cause marketing activations, for example:

- They drive strong awareness for your campaign in its first year.
- They establish it as an annual campaign.
- Over time, you can reduce your media investment as people recognise the activation and sometimes even pre-empt it.
- Alternatively, you can maintain or increase media spend to drive even more awareness and impact.

Shake Shack won a Gold Halo Award in 2014 for Best Social Service Campaign. Here are Shake Shack's business results from the campaign in May 2013:

- Shake Shack's vouchers for a free shake had a redemption rate of 44 per cent. That is a phenomenal result for voucher redemption. Remember, the voucher could only be redeemed on the customer's next visit.

- When customers returned to use their vouchers it drove incremental spend. On average, customers spent an additional $8 on their return visit.

- The campaign drove more trips to Shake Shack. There was an increase of 4 per cent of foot traffic to all Shake Shack restaurants compared to the previous month's traffic.

The Great American Shake Sale is an exceptionally good example of a cause marketing program that unifies Shake Shack staff and its customers towards a common cause. It is a blindingly simple campaign, but the way it has been structured and the attention to detail in its execution ensured that it has been highly effective.

As of 2016, this campaign has rolled out to three other markets – the UK stores have now run three annual shake sales, stores in Russia have run two shake sales and the Japanese stores launched their first campaign in 2016.

As a little addendum to this case study, I came across an interesting article. In 2014, an anonymous Shake Shack investor transferred $1 million worth of stock to Share Our Strength. The anonymous investor believed the stock could have a greater return on investment than many other traditional fundraising activities. Bill Shore, CEO of Share Our Strength reaffirmed this when he said, 'It looks like even a small equity stake in a growing company will enable us to do more to curb childhood hunger than some other forms of non-profit revenue generation.'

Innovation and progress – we're watching it unfold in front of our very eyes.

SIX KEY TAKE-OUTS FROM SHAKE SHACK'S APPROACH TO CAUSE MARKETING

1. *A credible partnership.* Food is the common and shared element in Shake Shack's offering and the No Kid Hungry program.

2. *Make the customer the hero.* By inviting customers to make the donation and rewarding them for it, Shake Shack acknowledged them as the heroes of the campaign. Shake Shack could so easily have offered to make a donation with every transaction, but this mechanic made their customers feel good about themselves and then recognised their actions with a reward.

3. *Internal engagement.* The company ensured its frontline staff were intimate with the details of the campaign and the cause they were supporting.

4. *Combine with new news.* Shake Shack connected the campaign with its new product flavours. This deepened the campaign's link with The Great American Bake Sale, making it fun and driving even more customer interest.

5. *Plan the customer journey.* Shake Shack planned the placement of its communication to ensure that the customer was aware and prepped before getting to the counter.

6. *Commitment and authenticity.* Shake Shack has committed to this partnership over a five-year period to date, making this an authentic partnership. The longevity of the program means customers and staff know it's a key part of what Shake Shack stands for. It builds the company's brand equity in being a community-centric business.

CHAPTER 8

PATAGONIA

Anti-consumerism makes a stand for the planet

Whenever you hear conversations around purpose-led brands, the name Patagonia is consistently raised. As a brand, it has a powerful mission that is central to everything the brand does.

Patagonia's mission statement is *'To build the best product, cause no unnecessary harm, use business to inspire and implement solutions to the environmental crisis.'*

Patagonia is an apparel company that grew out of a small company that made tools for climbers. It was founded in the US in 1973 by climber and environmentalist, Yvon Chouinard. Patagonia sells mainly sustainable outdoor clothing. The brand is not known for its low prices but it makes every effort to live by its mission statement and to ensure that its customers know about the value behind its products such as fair trade certified wages, traceable down, responsibly sourced merino wool and organic cotton.

In 1986, Patagonia committed to donating 10 per cent of its profits each year to small environmental groups that are working to save or restore habitat. The brand later increased its commitment to 1 per cent of sales or 10 per cent of profit, whichever is the greater number. Patagonia has kept to that commitment ever since.

Beyond donating a portion of the brand's annual profits, Patagonia also uses its marketing and business resources in support of activism. Years ago, after researching the materials used in the brand's products, it was discovered that the natural cotton fibre used in most of the sportswear was one of the biggest environmental villains. The pesticides used in the production of cotton resulted in pollution to the soil and fields. There was evidence that it also affected the health of field-workers. By 1996, all of Patagonia's sportswear was made with 100 per cent organic cotton and has been ever since.

ANTI-CONSUMERISM MARKETING

In November 2011, Patagonia led the marketing world in an unexpected piece of advertising that was timed to coincide with America's Black Friday. In case you're not familiar with Black Friday, it is the day following Thanksgiving in the US. It is widely regarded as the first day of the Christmas shopping season and, for that reason, retailers roll out big discounts and offers to entice shoppers to purchase from their stores, both online and in-store. In recent years, Black Friday has become known as a frenzy for shoppers, with store opening hours extended and people camping out and lining up to get the best deals. In some ways, it has come to stand for consumerism at its worst. From a retailer perspective, it's the busiest trading day of the year.

Patagonia's print advertisement, featuring one of its jackets, led with a bold headline 'DON'T BUY THIS JACKET'. The advertisement copy went on to explain the environmental cost of the R2 Jacket, one of their most popular pieces of apparel.[1]

'The environmental cost of everything we make is astonishing,' the advertisement read. It continued:

> 'Consider the R2 Jacket shown, one of our best sellers. To make it required 135 litres of water, enough to meet the daily needs (three glasses a day) of 45 people. Its journey from its origin as 60% recycled polyester to our Reno warehouse generated nearly 20 pounds of carbon dioxide, 24 times the weight of the finished product. This jacket left behind, on its way to Reno, two-thirds [of] its weight in waste.

> 'And this is a 60% recycled polyester jacket, knit and sewn to a high standard; it is exceptionally durable, so you won't have to replace it as often. And when it comes to the end of its useful life we'll take it back to recycle into a product of equal value. But, as is true of all the things we can make and you can buy, this jacket comes with an environmental cost higher than its price.'

The ad concludes:

> 'There is much to be done and plenty for us all to do. Don't buy what you don't need. Think twice before you buy anything. Go to *patagonia.com/CommonThreads*, take the Common Threads Initiative pledge and join us in the fifth R, to reimagine a world where we take only what nature can replace.'

The Rs referred to in the ad are part of a partnership Patagonia established with its consumers to consume less – a pledge to reduce, repair, reuse, recycle and reimagine. According to Patagonia's founder and owner, Yvon Chouinard, 'The Common Threads Initiative addresses a significant part of today's environmental problem – the footprint of our stuff. This program first asks customers to not buy something if they don't need it. If they do need it, we ask that they buy what will last a long time – and to repair what breaks, reuse or resell whatever they don't wear any more. And, finally, recycle whatever's truly worn out. We are the first company to ask customers to take a formal pledge and be partners in the effort to reduce consumption and keep products out of the landfill or incinerator.'[2]

Talk about brave and progressive! No wonder Patagonia customers are almost cult-like in their loyalty to the brand.

For Black Friday 2013, Patagonia took the idea further when it launched its Worn Wear program. The program offered a series of events where repair technicians and brand ambassadors taught Patagonia customers the skills to repair their 'tired well-loved clothing' (Patagonia or otherwise). People were also invited to share their stories on the Worn Wear blog or via Instagram. The brand now has a dedicated Instagram account for Worn Wear and publishes instruction guides on repairing Patagonia products.

One of the things I love about Patagonia is that the brand doesn't play by the rules of business.

In the Spring of 2014, Patagonia took the program on the road in a bio-diesel wagon with a solar-powered camper shell. The Worn Wear mobile tour started in California and stopped at retail sites, farmers' markets and coffee shops across the country before ending in Boston. Apart from staff doing repairs and showing people how to do their own repairs, the brand brought along some fun on tour including food, drinks and live music.

For a brand that lives and breathes its mission the way Patagonia does, storytelling is a great vehicle. A 30-minute documentary called *Worn Wear* was launched as part of the program. It's a film about used clothes. Laugh you might, but it's actually compelling to watch.

Patagonia also has an active YouTube channel that features original documentary shorts entitled *Stories We Wear*.

CONTENT MARKETING – A LESSON IN SIMPLICITY

For marketers today who are trying to understand how to use content marketing to promote their brand, Patagonia offers a lesson in simplicity. Stop trying to promote your brand. Instead, imagine what happens if your brand stands for something. If your brand has a strong authentic cause at its core then your cause becomes your content. Get it right and what will happen next is that your own customers – your tribe – will take up your story themselves. They'll start promoting your stories and with your stories, your brand.

Outside of content marketing, when you look at the Worn Wear program holistically, it offers up an extraordinary example of how Patagonia is using its principles as the foundation for engaging marketing that spans content, experience, retail and customer service.

It's a funny situation for Patagonia. Despite the brand's anti-consumerism stance in its marketing, sales have never been stronger. During the Worn Wear campaign, while industry-wide sales on Black Friday rose 2.3 per cent over the previous year, Patagonia's direct Black Friday sales rose 42 per cent. Online, the company saw a 61 per cent increase in consumer activity and the campaign generated more than half a billion media impressions.

DOES THIS MEAN PATAGONIA IS 'GREENWASHING'?

Greenwashing is the practice of making a misleading or unsubstantiated claim about the environmental credentials of a product. This isn't a criticism that is levelled at Patagonia and I don't believe it is one that would stand anyway. Patagonia goes to great lengths to live and breathe its mission. The brand involves activists and educators in its campaigns and part of the value is to get their customers and the wider market thinking more deeply about the impact their purchases have on the environment. Patagonia doesn't pretend to have all the answers but it is transparent in its efforts to be true to its mission.

PATAGONIA AUSTRALIA – THE DOUBLE DOWN

Here in Australia, Patagonia strives to live by the company's mission. In 2016, it ran a brand campaign that promoted fundraising for grassroots environmentalism.

The Double Down is a matched donation campaign where crowd-funded donations to six grassroots environmental groups were matched dollar-for-dollar by Patagonia, up to a combined total of $100,000.

The six groups fundraising through The Double Down work across Australia and Bali addressing a diverse range of environmental issues, each fundraising for a specific project:

- *Australian Marine Conservation Society* was fundraising to send an independent delegation of scientists and stakeholders to the World Heritage Committee meeting in Poland to give an independent voice to the Great Barrier Reef.

- *Southwest Marine Debris Clean Up* was boating into the remote Southwest wilderness of Tasmania to remove and study marine debris washed onto the area's beaches.

- *Lock the Gate Alliance* was fundraising to mobilise the local community to protect the farmland, vineyards and wilderness of the Margaret River region from unconventional gas exploration.

- *3000 Acres* was raising funds to build a large-scale community garden in Melbourne.

- *Seed Indigenous Youth Climate Network* was sending young Aboriginal and Torres Strait Islanders into remote Northern Territory communities to inform and mobilise locals against fossil fuel and gas extraction on their traditional lands.

- *Project Clean Uluwatu* is a group that was started by expat surfers to deal with wastewater and hard rubbish at Bali's famous surf break. The project was fundraising to hand control of the group over to local Balinese surfers.

The campaign was hosted on the crowdfunding platform Pozible. Patagonia took an omnichannel approach to the campaign with in-store communication utilising storyboards on each of the six environmental group projects. An ipad in each of Patagonia's stores enabled customers to explore the stories of each of the groups in more depth and social media also allowed the public to engage with the content.

The content strategy was an important part of the campaign and Patagonia created the content for each of the groups, ensuring consistent quality and exposure, so that there was a level playing field. Short videos were designed to be shared online, telling the story of each group and its issue while also pitching its project.

The groups themselves rallied their supporters to unlock the full benefit of the match campaign. While Patagonia Australia doesn't highlight this next point, and was probably not driven by it, this mechanic does have the benefit of promoting Patagonia to a group of supporters that may not otherwise have been exposed to the Patagonia brand and their proposition.

The campaign was a success. The final fundraising figure raised was $125,000. Six grassroots environmental groups were given high quality exposure through all of Patagonia's channels as well as through the Pozible community. Patagonia also promoted its brand through Pozible and through the supporter networks of each of the six participating groups.

One of the things I love about Patagonia is that the brand doesn't play by the rules of business. Patagonia creates its own rules. That's the kind of courage that attracts cult-like followers.

Patagonia refers to itself as an activist company. In its own words, the brand sets out its beliefs and its very reason for being:

'We believe the environmental crisis has reached a critical tipping point. Without commitments to reduce greenhouse gas emissions, defend clean water and air, and divest from dirty technologies, humankind as a whole will destroy our planet's ability to repair itself. At Patagonia, the protection and preservation of the environment isn't what we do after hours. It's the reason we're in business and every day's work.'

SIX TAKE-OUTS FROM PATAGONIA'S APPROACH TO CAUSE MARKETING

1. *Authenticity.* Stand for something and do something about it.

2. *Purpose and commitment.* This goes hand in hand with the previous point. Own your purpose and make it part of the very being of your brand.

3. *Transparency.* You might not always get it right but if
    you're authentic and transparent and you continually
    strive to improve, the market will support you.

4. *Educate.* Use your brand assets to spread the word and
    make it easy for people to find information on the cause
    and what your brand is doing to support it.

5. *Experiences.* Offer experiences to enable people to be
    a part of your activism.

6. *Tell stories and allow people to tell their stories.*
    Become a channel for the cause.

---

1   http://www.patagonia.com/blog/2011/11/dont-buy-this-jacket-black-friday-and-the-
    new-york-times/
2   http://www.prnewswire.com/news-releases/patagonia-launches-common-threads-
    initiative-a-partnership-with-customers-to-consume-less-129372068.html

CHAPTER 9

REI

#OptOutside

Let's say you're a marketer who is responsible for a brand in a category where another brand in the same category has established its credentials as a purpose-led brand. Perhaps you think you'll be accused of taking a 'me-too' position if you try to establish a cause or purpose-led approach for your brand. Perhaps you think the market is too small for two purpose-led brands in one category.

This next example demonstrates why that thinking is wrong and suggests that it's more to do with how you go about it.

REI, originally known as Recreational Equipment Inc., is an American retail and outdoor recreation business. It's a co-operative that sells sporting goods, camping gear, travel equipment and clothing. It also happens to sell Patagonia clothing and if you read the previous chapter, you'll know just how much of an environmental-led, purpose-driven brand Patagonia is.

So, it was very interesting to see REI take a high-profile purpose-led approach during Black Friday in 2015.

BRAVE MARKETING: TAKING A STAND AGAINST AN ESTABLISHED NORM

What REI did in 2015 was go against the popular tide. In the lead-up to Black Friday, REI announced that it would be closing all of its 143 stores (including its online store) on Black Friday, giving all of its staff a paid day of leave and encouraging customers and staff to get away from the shopping frenzy and head outside to enjoy the outdoors, the beautiful national parks, rivers and mountains. REI encouraged people to enjoy the fresh air and the exhilaration of outdoor experiences, 'To find balance in the simple; peace in the quiet.'

Jerry Stritzke, REI's president, wrote a letter to REI's 5.5 million members quoting outdoor visionary John Muir who said in 1901:

'thousands of tired, nerve-shaken, over-civilized people are beginning to find out that going to the mountains is going home.'

Stritzke continued:

'As a member-owned co-op, our definition of success goes beyond money. We believe that a life lived outdoors is a life well lived and we aspire to be stewards of our great outdoors. We think that Black Friday has gotten out of hand and so we are choosing to invest in helping people get outside with loved ones this holiday season, over spending it in the aisles. Please join us and inspire us with your experiences. We hope to engage millions of Americans and galvanize the outdoor community to get outside.'

The campaign launched with a memo to all REI staff and a print advertisement in *The New York Times*. In-store point of sale and large outdoor banners introduced people to the planned closure in advance. Television advertisements introduced the campaign name and hashtag #OptOutside, which later drove the creation of a meme generator that encouraged users to share images and videos of their own outdoor experiences.

A #OptOutside website featured stunning mountain photography and a list of hiking trails. Another feature was a partnership with a geo-mapping service that designed a mobile site, which helped less experienced outdoor enthusiasts find appropriate locations in their area to enjoy the natural world.

Public relations (PR) activity drove the message out to the media and the response was incredible – #OptOutside started trending immediately. Social media mentions rose 7,000 per cent with 2.7 billion PR impressions in 24 hours.

To rally outdoor enthusiasts, REI created outdoor camping kits, leveraging the tradition of eating Thanksgiving leftovers, by including freeze-dried Thanksgiving leftovers in the kits. These kits were sent to chosen influencers in the hiking and biking communities.

BEING TRUE TO ITS PURPOSE

REI had two key objectives in its sights for this campaign:

1. To reinforce its brand identity and link it back to its purpose, which was neatly embedded in the opening frame of the TVC – 'Outdoor retailer REI exists to get people outside'.
2. To encourage more people to shop in its stores in the short term.

According to the head of strategy from the agency responsible for the campaign, REI was crystal clear that this wasn't a stunt to drive sales. The company wasn't tracking the campaign based on a hope that people would buy more the following day. It was simply being true to its purpose and, commercially, playing the long game.

The campaign led to a significant rise in membership of REI's co-operative. This is considered far more important than any single sales increase given the co-operative model in which customers double as both employees and owners of the company.

A large part of this campaign was the internal buy-in of the employees of REI. Employee buy-in was considered by REI to be just as important as the advertisements to the viewing public. As one of the REI executives said:

> 'even if no one else in the world cares, that's 12,000 employees who get to spend the day outside with the people they love, not thinking about how to get to the store.'

However, something unexpected happened. Over 150 businesses followed REI's lead and closed their stores for Black Friday. State Parks opened their gates for free. Media articles picked up the sentiment and started asking whether REI's Black Friday closure could spark an anti-consumerist revolution.

Overall, in 2015, #OptOutside earned 6.7 billion media impressions, 1.2 billion social impressions and, most importantly, inspired 1.4 million people to spend their day outdoors.

From a big picture perspective, commercially, it appears to have paid off. Despite closing for the biggest trading day of the year, REI reported these results for the year-end following the 2015 #OptOutside campaign:

- A 9.3 per cent increase in revenue
- A 7 per cent increase in comparable store sales
- A 23 per cent uplift in digital sales
- The co-operative group announced that more than one million new members joined the company.

It was a brave campaign from REI and its agencies and marketing partners. It was duly recognised when it went on to win the Titanium Grand Prix at Cannes the following year.

BUILDING THE MOVEMENT IN 2016

For its 2016 campaign, REI continued its now celebrated #OptOutside program. The brand's aim was to build on the movement and to make the program a post-Thanksgiving tradition. The growing number of retailers that decided to join REI and close their stores for Black Friday made this huge goal possible. In 2016, 275 national and local organisations, including some branded stores, officially teamed up with REI to back the #OptOutside movement.

Among these partners was Subaru, a brand that, like REI, is a sponsor of the National Park Foundation and the National Parks Service Centennial which turned 100 years old in 2016. As part of its effort, Subaru committed to dispatching a fleet of cars to take shelter pets out of their cages for romps in the wilderness. It also sent shuttles to New York City to take pet parents and their dogs into the great outdoors.

REI's CEO said that the 2016 campaign took on a life of its own, with people who built their lives around the outdoors really embracing the idea of reclaiming Black Friday. He said:

> '#OptOutside should be a platform for the non-profits and public servants who are on the front lines of the outdoor community... That's why, from today onward, we're going to lift them up as the official spokespeople for #OptOutside.'

With 1.4 million people participating in the first year of the campaign (measured by the number of people who posted #OptOutside on their social media on the day), REI wanted to up the ante and find ways of getting more people outside on Black Friday.

As a marketer, it's worth considering that for a moment. Even as a business without your marketing hat on, just consider this – you're investing your marketing dollars in trying to get as many people as possible to get outdoors and enjoy the beauty of nature and you're helping them do it. Consider the social impact of that, with the average American purportedly spending 90 per cent of their time indoors. If brands can make a dent by lowering the percentage of time spent indoors that impact will be felt positively in numerous ways.

The 2016 campaign was refreshed with a playful theme that invited others to join in with #OptOutside by asking the audience 'Will you go out with me?' The energetic TVC showed #OptOutsiders frolicking on bikes, rollerblading, paddling in canoes and kayaks, swimming in rivers, hiking mountain trails and enjoying the snow. It was a true call to embrace the fun and energy of the great outdoors.

The 2016 campaign also made good on its goal to get more people outside by featuring a GPS-enabled mobile website which debuted an outdoor activity finder. This targeted people who weren't so familiar with what their outdoor options were. Visitors to the site could search by area or by activity. The site also offered classes and events for those who wanted to learn or improve their skills. Naturally, it also featured the clothing and equipment that REI sells, to go with the activities.

76 per cent of customers around the world say it's okay for brands to support good causes and make money at the same time.

Make no mistake, this program from REI is nothing short of courageous. Most big retailers wouldn't even consider closing their doors on the nation's biggest trading day of the year. Some retailers are even considering whether to open on Thanksgiving.

From the many articles I've read on this program, it wouldn't haven't been possible without the full support of the company's CEO. This is a characteristic I frequently hear of most successful cause campaigns. Get the CEO on board and fully supportive early – it will not only unlock the efforts of people and departments across your business, but it will also demonstrate the sincerity behind your campaign, when your CEO is prepared to invest his or her own brand and reputation.

Some will criticise the efforts of REI and Patagonia for leveraging an anti-consumerism message to drive increased sales and patronage of their brands. I strongly disagree with those criticisms. We live in a consumer society. That is a reality of our global economies.

An inordinate amount of money is spent by businesses to get people – consumers – to buy into their brand. What both REI and Patagonia have done is to take a stand on an issue that is highly relevant to their category. They have used their marketing might to drive awareness of that cause and build a movement around it. In doing so, they are reawakening feelings and a belief about what is truly important to people in this world. I call that responsible marketing. I have no problem with brands like that profiting from marketing in that way and I'm not alone in this thinking.

According to Edelman:[1]

> *'69 per cent of Australians think it's okay for brands to support good causes and make money at the same time.'*

Globally, that figure is higher. I suspect that is due to global markets in the research being further down the track in cause marketing than Australia.

'76 per cent of customers around the world say it's okay for brands to support good causes and make money at the same time.'[2]

There will be naysayers and critics – there always are. But be assured, these critics are in the minority. Arguably, as a marketer, if you don't have any critics, you're probably not causing much of a ripple. Sadly, some marketers respond to fear of criticism by dialling down what started as a brilliant idea. Too many end up being part of a collective that contributes irrelevant and empty 'puffery' into the universe. We're all guilty of that at some point in our careers.

I believe as marketers our job is to create ripples – ripples of action and impact. Sometimes, some brands create tidal waves of change. Those are the brands we should applaud and emulate.

When interviewed in 2016 by *Fortune* magazine, REI's CEO Jerry Stritzke fondly remembered his first #OptOutside Black Friday in 2015. While most retail executives are focused on making sure their operations are running smoothly on that day, Stritzke went for a hike with his three-year-old grandson. He says he has a picture of the two of them walking down a trail with his grandson holding a hiking stick in his hand.

'I had a wonderful experience and created a wonderful memory, and I'm looking to do the same this year,' he said.

FIVE TAKE-OUTS FROM REI'S APPROACH TO CAUSE MARKETING

1. *Be brave.* Take a stand on something that is relevant to your category or your audience.

2. *Be sincere.* Create a movement for change. Feed and build that movement beyond your own business benefits.

3. *Be collaborative.* Seek out like-minded partners to build the movement.

4. *Be helpful.* How can you help people get on board?

5. *Be committed.* Think beyond campaigns. Think big.

---

1   http://blog.edelman.com.au/2012/07/05/edelman-launches-goodpurpose-2012-with-australian-data/

2   Edelman, 2012, 'Edelman 2012 goodpurpose® Study', available at: http://www.edelman.com/insights/intellectual-property/good-purpose/

CHAPTER 10

MJAU AND WHISKAS

Cat saves cat

Some of the best things in the world have come out of Sweden – ABBA, Ikea, *The Girl with the Dragon Tattoo* book series, H&M and Absolut Vodka – and now, a cause marketing case study to add to that list. I only came across this recently as I was researching the Whiskas Big Cat case study for the World Wildlife Fund (WWF). Both campaigns launched at similar times, so it's not clear which one may have inspired the other. For fairness sake, I'll share the highlights of both.

SWEDEN: MJAU AND TETRA PAK – CAT HELPS CAT

Lantmännen Doggy is a Swedish company that produces responsibly farmed cat and dog food. It was the first company in the world to sell canned cat food in Tetra Paks. Tetra Pak is another ingenuity that Sweden brought to the world, packing perishable food in recyclable packaging from responsible sources. We know Tetra Pak best for the milk cartons we buy here in Australia.

In 2013, Lantmännen Doggy's cat food brand, Mjau, teamed up with Tetra Pak. Together, they partnered with WWF to help save the tiger.

As much as the internet is awash with everyday videos, photos and memes of the common cat, their big-cat cousin – the tiger – is in very serious danger of extinction. Illegal hunting by poachers has had a debilitating effect on the world's tiger population. There are only 3,200 tigers left in the wild – 97 per cent less than 100 years ago when their numbers were estimated at 100,000.

Cat Helps Cat, as the Mjau and Tetra Pak mutual project was called, centred around a special Cat Helps Cat food box that was created especially for this campaign. With every purchase of the food box, a donation was made to WWF.

This method of turning a committed donation from a company into a transactional mechanic to drive sales of a brand is a proven technique in cause marketing

A key feature of this campaign was a special tiger sponsor program that the brand created. Led by the campaign spokesperson – a superior four-pawed cat activist called Malte – Cat Helps Cat invited the approximately 1.3 million domestic cats of Sweden to sponsor a tiger in the wild. In return for a monthly donation, they were rewarded with a pawprint keyring, enabling their owners to show off their proud cat's activism.

Malte the cat-activist led the communications on Mjau's social media platforms, spreading the word and engaging cat lovers all around Sweden. A communications and events calendar of activity was also developed to leverage all windows of opportunity to get the word out.

Word did get out, resulting in high engagement from cats, humans and some human celebrities. Mjau's Facebook page quickly increased to 96,000 fans. Its monthly reach was up to 2 million unique users and 100,000 interactions, making it one of the fastest growing pages in the country.

Earned media in print, television and radio reached 29 per cent of the Swedish population and over 104,000 Cat Helps Cat food boxes were sold.

Most importantly, every single one of the 3,200 tigers in the wild now has a cat sponsor who will care for them in the long run.

Now that is what I call 'Cat Power'.

WHISKAS' PROTECT A TIGER CAMPAIGN

In 2013, Mars in the UK launched a cause marketing campaign for its Whiskas cat food brand. The campaign was beautifully aligned with Whiskas' TVC called 'Big Cat Little Cat' which showed footage of tiger cubs playing outdoors, then morphing into kittens coming home through the cat flap, highlighting that there's a big cat in every little cat. The tagline 'nurture their nature' completed the metaphor.

Launched as a fully integrated through-the-line campaign, it included a new campaign-specific TVC which highlighted the plight of the tiger and the connection between big cats and little cats, building on the theme of the Whiskas TVC. The advertisement explained that consumers could help by buying specially marked packs of Whiskas.

The campaign ran on 16 million Whiskas products, featuring eye-catching imagery of a Bengal tiger in its natural habitat. The call to action stated, 'Help protect a tiger' and invited consumers to buy Whiskas products to help raise up to £500,000 in donations for WWF's Tiger's Alive program. It was a simple transactional mechanic in which 3 pence was donated from each specially marked pack sold.

This method of turning a committed donation from a company into a transactional mechanic to drive sales of a brand is a proven technique in cause marketing, which engages consumers by enabling them to feel empowered and part of something bigger.

Whiskas' funding had a specific focus on WWF's work in the Terai Arc region of Nepal, which is one of the tiger's few remaining strongholds. To amplify the campaign and further drive awareness of the plight of the tiger, Whiskas funded a short film that was made in partnership with WWF. This funding was provided over and above their cause marketing donation.

Today, Whiskas' partnership with WWF stands strong as they work together to help tigers thrive. The program has also been rolled out by Mars to other European markets in Germany, Switzerland, Ireland and Belgium, with more markets to follow.

The Whiskas website captures the commitment the brand has to the cause and the results it has achieved thus far:

> 'Together, Whiskas® and WWF will provide increased protection in key habitats, working towards WWF's aim to double wild tiger numbers by 2022. We'll also focus on protecting tigers in the Terai Arc region of Nepal. It's one of the few remaining strongholds for this magnificent species, home to around 200 adult tigers.
>
> Our partnership with WWF began in 2013 and with your help we have raised over £600,000. This money has been used to provide the following:
>
> - 17 new community based anti-poaching units comprising 94 members
> - Solar panels to equip the guard posts with an electricity supply
> - Motorbikes to enable enforcement agencies to cover larger areas in a shorter space of time

- Search lights, tents, life-jackets for river crossings on patrol and bicycles.'

When I attended a global cause marketing conference in Chicago in 2014, there was a speaker from Mars UK, the parent company of Whiskas. In his presentation, he shared his company's experience in developing a research project into cause marketing. Mars wanted to identify how to create great campaigns that build brand value and growth. It tested a range of cause campaigns on its brands using different cause and communication strategies and it evaluated those campaigns using non-cause marketing campaigns as their benchmark. One of the cause campaigns in the research project was the Whiskas Protect a Tiger campaign.

The speaker shared five key insights that were formed from the research project:

1. Cause marketing is great for creating in-store events. It's a strategic and emotional winner with trade partners and in-store staff.
2. If you communicate the campaign 'on-pack', make sure the brand packaging is still identifiable so that consumers shopping in the category looking for the brand they usually buy can easily identify it.
3. Amplify your campaign. The speaker specifically highlighted the success of the Whiskas Protect a Tiger campaign, attributing the media amplification as a key success component.
4. Thirty-second TVCs are too constrained to unlock the full value of a cause campaign as they provide insufficient time for you to create tension then introduce the cause partner and the nature of the partnership.
5. Replicate success to get the cost benefits, e.g. roll out to other markets or roll out the program annually.

CHAPTER 11

ALLSTATE

The Purple Purse program

Allstate is the second largest personal lines insurance company in the US. The company offers insurance on cars, homes, content, life and roadside. Giving back has been one of the company's guiding principles and it has been doing this for 60 years in numerous ways through the Allstate Foundation.

With a philosophy that home should always be a safe place to go, the Allstate Foundation is a long-term supporter of victims of domestic abuse and the company often addresses issues of domestic violence and financial abuse.

The insight behind Allstate's support of this cause is that the number one reason women in abusive relationships can't 'just leave' is because they're being financially abused.

In 2011, the Allstate Foundation set out to drive awareness of this issue by launching the Purple Purse program. The Allstate Purple Purse program aimed to make it more 'fashionable' to talk about domestic violence and issues of financial control, sabotage and exploitation that trap women in exploitative relationships.

Allstate's 2012 campaign aimed to not only get people to talk about the subject but also to inspire conversation and show that Allstate is a leader in driving overall awareness about domestic violence.

The Allstate Foundation offered $175,000 to YWCA for programs to help domestic violence survivors. However, Allstate didn't just provide the cash up-front, it used a transactional mechanic to make up the donation amount. People had to 'pass' virtual and physical purses (filled with information about domestic violence) to one another with each pass triggering a small donation. The campaign reached its goal in the first two weeks and the total amount garnered was $250,000.

There were 500 physical purses stuffed with information about domestic violence circulated – each purse was passed between thousands of people throughout the campaign. The purses were distributed across the country to key stakeholders such as 75 Allstate agents, advocates for educating people about domestic violence and journalists.

Today, the Allstate Foundation Purple Purse program talks about making the invisible visible. The Foundation states its position as bringing abuse out of the shadows and using financial empowerment to break the cycle of domestic violence.

Social impact results[1] published to date include:

- More than $50 million invested in ending domestic violence.
- Nearly 800,000 survivors have been supported to take steps toward stronger, happier, domestic violence-free lives.
- More than 8,600 service providers trained to help deliver best-in-class financial literacy and asset building programs for domestic violence survivors in all 50 states.

Given this program is run through the Allstate Foundation – the company's charitable arm – there will be no value attached to any commercial benefits deriving it. Regardless, I thought it was a good example to highlight in this book given the way the company actively engaged the public and drove awareness of a problem that is all too often hidden.

How would you value the brand awareness of Allstate's association with this powerful program?

FOUR TAKE-OUTS FROM ALLSTATE'S APPROACH TO CAUSE MARKETING

1. *Drive credibility* by aligning your brand with a cause that is relevant to your product offering or philosophy (home should be a safe place to go) and by making a long-term commitment to the cause.

2. *Identify a specific issue to address.* In this case, addressing financial abuse and exploitation enables the Allstate Foundation to own and drive real impact in this area.

3. *Themes* can be a good way to engage your target audience by speaking a language that talks to them. In Allstate's case, it linked the cause to fashion.

4. *A transactional mechanic doesn't always have to be linked to purchase*, it can be linked to a transactional action such as passing on a purse.

---

1   https://www.allstatefoundation.org/domestic_violence.html

CHAPTER 12

DULUX

The Dulux Surf Club Project

Dulux Weathershield paint offers long-life protection from all Australian weather conditions. The Dulux Promise guarantees that Dulux Weathershield will protect your home for as long as you live in it.

It's a pretty bold claim given that parts of this beautiful land of ours are subject to some pretty harsh weather elements. However, Dulux found a compelling way to bring this claim to life and to test it, visibly and publicly.

In 2011, Dulux launched its partnership with Surf Lifesaving Australia (SLSA) with the Dulux Surf Club Project. The project enabled every one of the 300+ surf lifesaving clubs in Australia to be repainted with Dulux interior and exterior paint so that while our surf lifesavers are out saving lives, Dulux is helping to ensure their surf clubs and club houses are protected.

Surf Lifesaving Australia is a not-for-profit organisation, as are each of the individual surf lifesaving clubs, so it is reliant on the support of its partners to fund the critical work it does in the community.

A CREDIBLE CAUSE PARTNERSHIP

The partnership was a strategic alignment made in heaven. Surf lifesaving club buildings are subject to the harshest weather elements in the country. The project made for a powerful and confident statement about the protective benefits of Dulux Weathershield paint.

The local surf lifesaving clubs themselves are also at the heart of Australia's coastal local communities. They're a hub for families and people of all ages who enjoy our world-famous beaches. There is also a lot of goodwill directed towards surf lifesaving clubs so a brand that aligns with the local surf club, and does it in such a unique and authentic way, is surely going to get some goodwill value out of the partnership.

PRODUCT DONATIONS DRIVE A POWERFUL BRAND MESSAGE

Let's look at what was involved in the project.

As a sponsor, Dulux pays a sponsorship or licensing fee in order to be able to use SLSA's assets and logo in any of its communications. There is also a royalty arrangement whereby a percentage of every product sold goes to SLSA.

Over and above that, through the promise of the Dulux Surf Club Project, each individual surf lifesaving club is invited to register and receive Dulux paint to use on both the interior and exterior of the surf club buildings. Based on a three-year renewal of the partnership signed in 2016, each registered club is entitled to 100 litres of paint each year for the length of the three-year partnership.

As at February 2017, 150 clubs have completed painting their buildings and 60 are now re-painting their buildings.

While there is no expectation for Dulux to provide the manpower to paint the clubs, some of their sales teams volunteer to get out in their local communities to help with the painting. Whether it's intended or not, that is a powerful relationship-builder between locals and a representative of the Dulux brand, which can't be bad for the goodwill directed towards the brand.

Beyond the actual community project, Dulux leverages this partnership through its brand communications. The brand's TVC showcases the Dulux Surf Club Project as testament of the efficacy of the Dulux Weathershield protection promise.

STRONG BRAND HEALTH RESULTS

The program has now been running for six years and there are no signs of Dulux moving away from this partnership. When I spoke to a member of Dulux's marketing team about the company's future plans for the partnership, he said that Dulux was in this for the long term.

Dulux's commitment to this project is strong – why wouldn't they be committed? As a marketing strategy, it has been enormously successful. Brand health metrics show a significant increase since the program began and research shows that people place huge value on the brand's benefit of 'protection from the Australian sun'.

It's not just brand health that benefits from this program. Dulux has managed to land the triple win: brand health, sales increase and social contribution. Every time Dulux airs the TVC, the company sees an increase in sales.

What's more, over the last four years, Dulux has been voted the number one paint brand and one of the top ten brands overall in *Reader's Digest's* Trusted Brands survey. Australians said that Dulux is a well-known Australian brand that stands for quality, the best results, reliability and consistency.

I've written extensively about cause marketing as an incredible strategy that enables brands to do well by doing good and this project is a perfect example of this.

THE FUTURE

Moving forward, the Dulux brand team see the opportunity to move deeper with this program – to engage more with local surf clubs and to also look at leveraging the program through their trade partners, both their retail partners and their trade painter network.

Based on this insight, I can only see this program getting stronger as the depth of the brand's engagement with the surf lifesaving community grows.

I believe this program will truly be looked at over time as one of those iconic brand campaigns that stands out as an example for brand marketers to celebrate and emulate. It's hitting that mark already. When I highlight this campaign as an example of brilliant cause and community marketing in meetings with brand marketers, there is unanimous agreement. I think we all wish that we had some involvement with such an intelligent and successful campaign. Clearly, I love this program. It has all the ingredients for success.

THREE KEY INGREDIENTS IN THE SUCCESS OF THE DULUX SURF CLUB PROJECT

1. *Credibility:*
   - Dulux paint offers real value to the participating surf clubs. It would be a high cost to the clubs if they had to buy paint for themselves.

   - For Dulux Weathershield, there is no better way to bring their 'protection' benefit to life than through this program and by painting the buildings that are exposed to the very harshest Australian weather.

2. *Authenticity:*
   - The program offers a six-year partnership with an on-going commitment.

   - It is a partnership that is amplified authentically and emotively.

3. *Local and emotive:*
   - For a global brand, Dulux has hit a 'six' for delivering local relevance. Our surf clubs are iconic and a big part of the Australian identity, for people who live both on the coast and in-land.

   - The benefits of the program at a grassroots level – the involvement in our local communities – are obvious. However, by amplifying the program, Dulux is also showcasing our surf lifesaving clubs as a highly prized part of Australian culture. It's an incredibly emotive association that provides a big payoff for the brand.

CHAPTER 13

VIRGIN MOBILE

Making Mobile Better

Virgin Mobile is the young kid on the block in the Australian telecommunications industry. Facing up against the big and established players – Telstra, Optus and Vodafone – Virgin Mobile doesn't have the big budget of these competitor brands to invest in heavy media schedules. For that reason, and of course because it is part of the Virgin brand, the company needs to think differently in order to engage its market.

In July 2014, Virgin Mobile launched a campaign platform that clearly differentiated from its competitors and positioned the brand as leading-edge in terms of shaping the mobile experience for its Australian market.

The platform was centred on a new online hub *www.making-mobilebetter.com.au*. This hub was essentially the mothership for a series of 'Making Mobile Better' campaigns that were all based on making the mobile experience better for Virgin Mobile customers. The idea behind it came from the global Virgin purpose, 'to change the game for good'. The rise of mobile phones has created both positive and negative behaviours and outcomes. Making Mobile Better set out to turn some not-so-good behaviours into good outcomes.

The campaign launched with a 45-second TVC, featuring one of the stars of *Glee*, Jane Lynch. It was a funny, entertaining advertisement in which Jane highlights some of the silly ways we use our phones. By duplicating these behaviours without the aid of a mobile phone the commercial highlights just how crazy some of the things we do are, from social media posts and sharing selfies, to following and hashtagging.

#MEALFORAMEAL – TURNING A TRIVIAL ACTION INTO A POSITIVE DIFFERENCE

The first initiative Virgin Mobile launched was in August 2014 and was called #mealforameal. The idea came from the insight that people like to use their phone to take photos of beautiful meals and then share them via social media. The marketing team at Virgin Mobile zeroed in on making that trivial action a better experience for the user by partnering with not-for-profit food rescue service, OzHarvest.

According to OzHarvest, four million tonnes of food are wasted every year in Australia alone. We throw away food worth $8 billion annually and it goes straight to landfill.

Despite all of this food being wasted, two million Australians are reliant on food relief every year, with 90 per cent of Australian food relief agencies not able to meet demand for meals. It would seem that while we're sharing meals on Instagram, we're not sharing meals where they are really needed.

Through the #mealforameal campaign, every time someone snapped a photo of their food and posted it to social media with the accompanying hashtag, Virgin Mobile donated to OzHarvest so that it could deliver a meal to someone in need. The cost of delivering a meal at that time was just 50 cents.

Through this unique initiative, Virgin Mobile's aim was to combat hunger and food wastage by delivering meals to vulnerable Australians through OzHarvest. The brand set a huge goal of 400,000 meals snapped and delivered. The scale of the goal was set high deliberately because Virgin Mobile wanted to demonstrate an ongoing commitment to its partner, OzHarvest. For Virgin Mobile, #mealforameal was much more than just another marketing campaign, it was a genuine social campaign to drive impact.

To communicate the campaign, Virgin Mobile used social media, mobile media, online video, TV and contextual out-of-home (OOH) placements. Time-targeted messages across mobile explained the campaign. In addition, social media calls to take action formed an always-on messaging approach. All of the mobile media was complimented by media placements on TV, food court tables and transit areas where mobile usage often peaked.

The campaign generated a huge amount of social media chatter with Adriano Zumbo, George Calombaris, Matt Moran, Andrew Levins and even Jamie Oliver jumping on board through their own social media channels and encouraging their followers to get involved. And as part of a commercial partnership, the team from Gelato Messina even created a special flavour of gelato to get their customers behind the campaign.

Punching above its weight in social media performance and driving sales

The campaign strengthened the Virgin Mobile brand by leveraging the existing social behaviour of consumers to give back to society, bringing the brand's mission of 'making mobile better' to life. It also humanised the brand by demonstrating that Virgin supported its customers' desire to help those in need. This shifted the mobile phone provider from a commodity to a community asset. Public receptiveness to this was evident based on the number of meals donated, the number of positive comments received over social media, and increase in the brand's social followers.

The results from the campaign's first year were outstanding:

- 260,000 meals were provided
- On Facebook alone, #mealforameal achieved a 45.6 million reach
- On Twitter, there were 2,247 weekly brand interactions
- On Instagram there was an 18 per cent increase in followers with no spend
- Overall, there were 20+ million interactions across Facebook, Twitter and Instagram and 1.5 million views on the campaign's YouTube and Facebook native videos
- 7 per cent of social media users who saw the campaign interacted with it – a statistic that is 13 times higher than the industry standard engagement rate of 0.54 per cent.

#mealforameal year two

In 2015, Virgin Mobile wanted to scale out the initiative even further – so the brand took a different approach in the second year of the campaign. First, Virgin Mobile enlisted the help of Guillaume Brahimi, one of Australia's most celebrated French chefs who is known for his fine-dining techniques and impeccable standards. Then, using Brahimi to front the brand's communications, Virgin Mobile challenged Australians to get involved by posting everything they were eating – the good, the bad and the ugly, the unfiltered and un-styled, the 3am kebabs and the homemade spaghetti on toast, as well as their high quality, high-end meals.

The campaign featured two spoof cooking show films which were featured on the Making Mobile Better website, YouTube channel and across all of Virgin Mobile's owned channels.

The first spoof film showed Brahimi creating a blackened, toasted passionfruit soufflé, highlighting that disasters can happen even to the very best chefs. In the second spoof film, Brahimi gets real with his croque-monsieur recipe – the ultimate ham and cheese toastie.

Both films use humour to show that no matter what you're cooking and how you cook it, it's all about supporting a great cause.

In addition to its marketing of the OzHarvest partnership, Virgin Mobile looked internally, just as it tries to do for all of its cause marketing efforts. Staff at the company are entitled to one paid day per year to volunteer and many took the opportunity to volunteer with OzHarvest – preparing and delivering meals for people and families in need.

In another move, instead of giving its staff Christmas presents, Virgin Mobile donated meals to OzHarvest on behalf of their staff. These initiatives seem to be paying off as the company registers high employee net promoter score results year on year.

R U OK?DAY. ENCOURAGING CUSTOMERS TO REACH OUT TO SOMEONE WHO MAY BE STRUGGLING

The second initiative Virgin Mobile launched as part of its Making Mobile Better platform was its partnership with R U OK?Day.

R U OK? is a not-for-profit organisation whose vision is a world where we're all connected and protected from suicide. Based on the theory that suggests there is power in the simple question 'are you OK?', the organisation aims to encourage and equip everyone to regularly and meaningfully ask the people around them, 'are you OK?'.

Virgin Mobile's decision to be a 'conversation partner' of R U OK?Day highlighted the tendency of people to connect with others only through social media rather than in person or via a phone call. In 2014, launching the campaign in the lead up to R U OK?Day, Virgin Mobile encouraged people to reach out to people who may be struggling by calling and actually speaking to them on the phone. All Virgin Mobile customers were offered free calls on R U OK?Day. The campaign launched with a video of Virgin's founder, Sir Richard Branson, with paid OOH media following up.

Since the 2014 launch, Virgin Mobile has continued its partnership with R U OK?Day and offers free calls to its customers on the day. Virgin Mobile also reminds its customers via social media, email direct marketing (EDM) and SMS to reach out to someone and ask 'are you OK?'.

SMILING MINDS

In 2016, Virgin Mobile added another partner to continue its drive to Make Mobile Better. The brand partnered with Smiling Mind, a not-for-profit organisation that works to make mindfulness meditation accessible to everyone. The Smiling Mind app is used in schools by more than 18,000 educators and is also currently being used by more than 200 workplaces. The organisation's vision is to see mindfulness meditation on the national Australian Curriculum by 2020.

Virgin Mobile launched its cause marketing campaign with Smiling Mind in October 2016. To inspire people to make time for everyday meditation, the brands placed pod-like meditation chairs in Martin Place in Sydney, Federation Square in Melbourne and Queen Street Mall in Brisbane. Their goal was to illustrate that no matter where you are, even if you're in the middle of the city during your working day, it is feasible to take 10 minutes to yourself to practise a little mindfulness.

According to Virgin Mobile's CEO at the time, David Scribner:

> 'As a Virgin business, it's important we take responsibility for the products we sell, by reminding our customers of the benefits of taking a little time out for yourself each day. By partnering with Smiling Mind and their meditation app, we want to deliver a more genuine mobile phone experience for our customers that helps restore balance to their lives. Encouraging them to make mindfulness part of their daily mobile behaviour can do just that.'

FINDING PURPOSE AND CONNECTING WITH THEIR CUSTOMERS

Using credible cause partnerships that are brought to life through intelligent marketing activation ideas is a smart move for a small brand in a highly competitive category.

By helping its target audience to take action to do something good, Virgin Mobile has tapped into the powerful desire that people have to collaborate with brands to contribute positively to society.

According to research, 71 per cent of people believe that brands and consumers could do more to support good causes by working together and 63 per cent want brands to make it easier for them to make a positive difference[1].

What I love about Virgin Mobile's platform and these two campaigns is that the company is moving the conversation in the telecommunications category away from the usual value proposition of features and benefits. Instead, Virgin Mobile is branching out into rich and unique territory that aims to engage with people emotionally and authentically.

FIVE KEY TAKE-OUTS FROM VIRGIN MOBILE'S APPROACH TO CAUSE MARKETING

1. *Credible and authentic partnerships* will create positive engagement with customers and prospects.

2. *Enable collaboration.* Leverage existing behaviours and enable consumers to collaborate and participate.

3. *Refresh your platform.* #mealforameal made its second year of the campaign an opportunity for people to have fun.

4. *Set big long-term commitments.* This will enable your brand to cut-through the noise and deliver deeper social impact.

5. *A unique approach for the right cause* can attract celebrity endorsement and influence.

---

1 Edelman, 2012, 'Edelman 2012 goodpurpose® Study', available at: http://www.edelman.com/insights/intellectual-property/good-purpose/

According to research, 71 per cent of people believe that brands and consumers could do more to support good causes by working together.

CHAPTER 14

ANZ

Celebrating gender diversity

Banks and financial institutions are the bastions of conservatism – this campaign is anything but. This next case study is a world-class marketing campaign that embodies everything that is good about cause marketing.

ANZ has been a supporter of the Sydney Gay and Lesbian Mardi Gras since 2006. For any non-Australians reading this, the Sydney Gay and Lesbian Mardi Gras started as a protest march for the rights of the gay and lesbian community back in 1978. Over the years, it has become a global beacon and celebration of diversity, not to mention another excuse for Sydney to party (as if we need an excuse!). Its purpose now is to inspire the world to love each other by celebrating the power and beauty of diversity.

In 2014, ANZ became the inaugural principal partner for the festival. The bank set out to leverage its partnership with the Sydney Gay and Lesbian Mardi Gras to communicate ANZ's support for diversity, respect and inclusion – and to do so in a fun and meaningful way. The intended target market was not just the LGBTQIA+

community but also ANZ's own employees, prospective employees and consumers.

TURNING ATMs INTO DAZZLING GAYTMs!

Ten ATMs in central Sydney were each transformed into unique 'GAYTMs' for three weeks surrounding Mardi Gras. Each GAYTM celebrated a part of gay and lesbian culture and was decorated individually with sequins, moustaches, rhinestones, leather, denim and fur. The GAYTMs also featured the following hashtags – *#hellosailor*, *#mo-town*, *#drag-it-up* and *#unicorn-dream* to encourage users to spread the word about each GAYTM. There was even a microsite created to tell each GAYTM's story. If you've not seen them, please do yourself a favour and check them out online – you won't regret it!

CASH OUT AND PROUD

Messages proclaiming 'Happy Mardi Gras' and 'Hello Gorgeous' were shown on the screens of the GAYTMs, which also dispensed rainbow coloured receipts with the message 'Cash out and proud'.

During the campaign period, ANZ donated all GAYTM operator fees to gay and lesbian charity organisation, Twenty10.

The campaign naturally lent itself to social media activity as people used the seeded hashtag *#GAYTM* along with hashtags of each of the individual GAYTM names to spread the word. The creation, installation and delighted public reactions to the GAYTMs became content across Instagram, YouTube, Flickr, Twitter and Facebook. The word 'GAYTM' neatly seeded itself into the social vernacular.

One of the aims of this campaign was to get Australia, and indeed the world, talking – to fuel a social conversation and, in doing so, spread three of ANZ's corporate values: diversity, inclusion and respect.

The campaign was a huge success with 62 million media impressions across 70 countries, with 90 per cent positive social sentiment. Media and bloggers didn't just report on the GAYTMs but also praised ANZ for making such a bold public statement. People commented through social feeds that they were proud ANZ customers or they would seriously consider switching to ANZ as a result of this campaign. The campaign also led people to seek out the GAYTMs which, of course, increased the donation amount.

The campaign delivered ANZ the highest engagement rate of all Australian banks across Facebook, Twitter and Instagram. It attracted thousands and thousands of new customers in New South Wales and staff feedback was outstanding. The campaign was awarded a Grand Prix for Outdoor at the 2014 Cannes Lions.

A CELEBRATION OF SHARED VALUES

ANZ's 2014 GAYTM campaign was bold, it was beautiful and it was clever. It was indeed a celebration of the LGBTQIA+ community and of the values the community shares with ANZ – support for diversity, respect and inclusion.

The popular GAYTMs were again rolled out in 2015 but in 2016, to mark the bank's 10th anniversary of supporting the Sydney Gay and Lesbian Mardi Gras, the marketing team at ANZ and their agency, Whybin/TBWA Group Melbourne, went one step further.

GAYNZ... AND PROUD

In 2016, ANZ took the theme of celebration to a whole new level. ANZ's Oxford Street branch – located at the heart of the Mardi Gras parade route in Darlinghurst, Sydney – transformed itself into GAYNZ, a fabulous and flamboyant representation of gayness the world has ever seen from a bank.

The result was a baroque-inspired celebration of LGBTQIA+ culture that featured hand-painted, crazy and wonderful murals, frescoes, a rose wall entrance, marble floors, pink poodle marble statues, chaise longues, stained glass and a pair of giant penguins in the foyer. The penguins paid homage to two emperor penguins from a Dutch zoo who coupled up and adopted and raised a baby penguin after its egg was abandoned by its mother.

In a first for a bank worldwide, ANZ also teamed up with Twitter to develop a rainbow flag emoji, which appeared whenever people hashtagged #*GAYNZ*.

GAYNZ stood proud for two weeks and the results were incredible. During that two-week period, ANZ had 7,000 visitors to the Oxford Street branch. On average, branches usually have 1,000 people visit during that same time period.

The campaign garnered 816 million media impressions and the number of new accounts opened at GAYNZ more than doubled.

As Pedestrian TV called it at the time, GAYNZ was 'a financial f@#*ing wonderland'.

A campaign like that takes courage. Full credit to the client team at ANZ and to the agency Whybin/TBWA Group Melbourne that had the courage to break the mould of conservative bank sponsorship activation campaigns.

For the team that worked on this campaign and the GAYTM campaigns before this, I can only imagine the incredible sense of pride they feel at what they achieved. This is the kind of campaign that transcends marketing. It's inspirational and I hope we see more of its kind in the near future.

2017 CAMPAIGN – HOLD TIGHT

In 2017, ANZ adopted a very different tone for its campaign in the run up to Mardi Gras. Research for the campaign, commissioned by ANZ, revealed that 94 per cent of Australians believe everyone should feel comfortable holding hands in public, regardless of sexual orientation or gender identity. However, the reality is that only 43 per cent of LGBTQIA+ Australians feel at ease doing so.

A video campaign was created that featured LGBTQIA+ couples highlighting their hesitance to hold hands in public. The advertisement features a range of scenes showing different couples enjoying time together in public places and holding each other's hands. But when other people in those public places notice them holding hands, they quickly pull away from each other. A tagline at the end of the video reads 'When you feel like letting go, #*holdtight*'.

It's an insightful and emotive piece of marketing which promotes ANZ's support of equality. It directly targets the LGBTQIA+ community as well as indirectly targeting the rest of the community with a very relatable scenario.

The campaign's launch also included a Twitter hashtag, which transformed into an emoji of two intertwined hands when used. ANZ offered attendees at both Sydney Mardi Gras and Auckland pride festivals custom wristbands which lit up when wearers held hands. The first of its kind, the wristband used infrared technology to detect proximity between its wearers.

It was a distinctive change of tone from the fun and flamboyant GAYTM and GAYNZ campaigns of previous years. Yet, from the discussions I viewed among some in the LGBTQIA+ community on social media, it seems to have absolutely hit the mark with some commenters highlighting that the video moved them to tears.

There is no doubt that ANZ's long-term support of the LGBTQIA+ community gave the brand permission to move to this next level of emotional support. ANZ has shown both leadership and sensitivity in how it has approached this partnership. ANZ is an incredible example of cause marketing that stands proudly on the global stage. It will be exciting to see how the partnership develops over time.

SEVEN TAKE-OUTS FROM ANZ'S APPROACH TO CAUSE MARKETING

1. Cause marketing can be fun, as well as poignant.

2. Build on your brand or company's values to strengthen your credibility, internally and externally.

3. A bold public statement will put you in the public eye. Make sure you can live up to scrutiny.

4. A celebration of your cause is a great unifier and a powerful way to drive social engagement.

5. Brave brands inspire proud customers and employees.

6. Long-term commitment to a cause builds rock-solid authenticity.

7. Refreshing your approach over time allows you to build a richer, deeper relationship with your constituents.

CHAPTER 15

BEN & JERRY'S

Brand activists

Ben & Jerry's is an ice cream company, which originated in the US in 1978. The company was started by two friends who opened their first ice cream shop in a renovated gas station in Burlington, Vermont. In 1979, Ben & Jerry's celebrated its one-year anniversary by holding the first-ever Free Cone Day – free scoops for all, all day long. The annual ice cream giveaway continues today in scoop shops around the world.

Social mission was an early development for the business. In 1985, the Ben & Jerry's Foundation was established to fund community-oriented projects.

In 2000, Ben & Jerry's became a wholly-owned subsidiary of Unilever. As part of the acquisition, a unique arrangement was made – an independent board of directors was created to provide leadership that was focused on preserving and expanding Ben & Jerry's social mission, brand integrity and product quality.

The following year, in 2001, Ben & Jerry's made a movie called *Citizen Cool*. It was a documentary about ordinary people making an impact in their communities. Ben & Jerry's celebrated the release of the movie with a new ice cream flavour inspired by movie treats, Concession Obsession.

Other campaigns followed and supported causes such as making a stand for the environment, encouraging people to get out and vote (that was as far back as 2004) and supporting fair trade efforts.

In Australia, one of Ben & Jerry's campaigns stands out for special mention – it is a campaign that really cemented the brand in the social activism category in this country.

In 2014, Ben & Jerry's partnered with World Wildlife Fund (WWF) and Australian Marine Conservation Society for the 'Fight for the Reef' campaign. At the heart of this campaign was an effort to engage consumers in the fight to protect the Great Barrier Reef and stop the dredging and dumping of sludge into the reef.

Ben & Jerry's partnered with the cause by embarking on a three-week national 'Fight for the Reef' Scoop Tour, travelling the east coast of Australia in a branded Ben & Jerry's van covered with the campaign message.

At every stop on the tour, Ben & Jerry's staff collected signatures, educated consumers on the threat through a bespoke arcade game and they captured photo testimonies, which were then shared straight onto Ben & Jerry's social media platforms. Along the way, they surprised and delighted fans with free ice cream by responding to Twitter requests and they even got five cows together for a final protest in Airlie Beach.

Ben & Jerry's achieved some fantastic results from the scoop tour:

- Over 45,000 free scoops of Ben & Jerry's ice cream were given out during the campaign
- Over 20,000 signatures were collected for the WWF Fight for The Reef petition
- Over 3,000 photos were shared on social media
- The campaign engaged in over 50,000 conversations.

The campaign received national media attention, including a feature on Channel 10's *The Project*.

The campaign was welcomed with enthusiasm from consumers, many of whom shared concerns over the threat to the Great Barrier Reef. However, not everyone was enthusiastic about Ben & Jerry's activism.

The Queensland government came out aggressively against the campaign. A handful of politicians accused Ben & Jerry's of using the campaign to spread 'lies and deceit' around the issue and they went on to propose a nationwide boycott of Ben & Jerry's as a consequence. They even went as far as referring the company to the Australian Competition and Consumer Commission (ACCC), accusing Ben & Jerry's of threatening the reputation of the reef and, consequently, costing tourism dollars and jobs.

The actions of the government arguably increased the profile of the Ben & Jerry's campaign, beyond anything their silence would have achieved, with national media exposure following the stoush between the Queensland government players and the activist brand. For its part, Ben & Jerry's kept its response to the attacks light with tweets such as 'I think my favourite *#benandjerrys* flavour is an apologetic politician' and 'National eat your bodyweight in Ben & Jerry's ice cream day. Who's with me?' appearing on the campaign website.

If you follow the media trail and, once you get past all the Queensland government outrage and puffery, the lead goes suddenly quiet. It appears the government threats were little more than hot air.

Through this campaign, Ben & Jerry's drew attention to an important public issue. The brand also drew attention to itself and cemented its reputation as a light-hearted social activist brand that isn't afraid to ruffle feathers. There is no doubt that this position has endeared the brand to many Millennial and Gen Z consumers, as much as the free scoops of ice cream also did.

SIX TAKE-OUTS FROM BEN & JERRY'S APPROACH TO CAUSE MARKETING

1. *Have fun with cause marketing.* If it suits your brand, you can also be a little cheeky!

2. *Become an educator for a cause.* It's a great way to attract interest and shares.

3. *Make your audience the heroes* by inviting them to sign a petition.

4. *Integrate free product samples* to convert new customers into advocates.

5. *Create photo opportunities* to leverage social content.

6. *Maintain your brand tone* even when government officials threaten you.

CHAPTER 16

CALTEX

Star Mart Wish Drive

In 2013, my business, Sunday Lunch, worked on what became known as the Star Mart Wish Drive. Caltex had been a client of ours for 16 years at that time and the company called on us to work collaboratively with its brand and media agencies to develop a cause marketing program in partnership with Make-A-Wish Australia.

Make-A-Wish is a not-for-profit organisation that grants wishes to seriously ill children. The impact that the wishes have on these young kids is incredibly positive, bringing real joy to the kids themselves as well as to their families.

Caltex chose Make-A-Wish as its cause partner based on a previous partnership it had with the Starlight Children's Foundation, which had been a long-standing and active partnership over many years starting in around 1999. Similar to Make-A-Wish, the Starlight Foundation works to brighten the lives of seriously ill children and their families.

Among some of Caltex's long-standing executives, there was a real desire to partner again with an organisation that worked in this area to help kids who were facing serious health challenges. I make this point because the credibility of this particular partnership isn't as visible as some of the other case studies I have shared in this book. It doesn't mean though that the choice of partner doesn't stand up to rigour.

For the Caltex team that was responsible for the inception of the Make-A-Wish partnership, the desire to return to working with a partner such as the Starlight Children's Foundation ran deep. The partnership with the Starlight Children's Foundation had been very active as Caltex staff and franchisees were invested in fundraising and building awareness of a very important cause. Naturally, the partnership was also a fit with Caltex's customers, many of whom are families with young children and who would feel empathy towards the cause.

When we were briefed on this project, it soon became clear that it was one that I would identify as a 'passion project'. There was originally no budget to fund it, but the retail marketing team wanted to look at the possibility of doing something and finding a way to fund it. Given the lack of budget, we looked at what assets Caltex had that could deliver value. Caltex has a huge footprint of sites, with millions of people coming through its store doors every month. This was a clear asset and we identified very quickly the value of that asset as a fundraising vehicle.

The core proposition invited motorists and convenience store customers to 'Join the Star Mart Wish Drive' and to 'Help make wishes come true.' In its first year, the campaign ran for four weeks and there were multiple ways customers could get involved. The campaign invited customers to donate at least $2 to receive a sticker with an 'I love granting wishes' message that recognised their support of the cause.

Caltex got many of its suppliers on board – products that Caltex sold offered to donate a portion of sales to Make-A-Wish. The products were specially marked so that customers could easily identify them. Caltex extended the offer to its own products so that sales of Caltex Delo lubricants and Star Mart milk or bread also donated a percentage of sales.

In order to maximise the fundraising effort, a specific campaign day was designated and it was named 'Wish Drive Day'. It enabled the franchisees and company-owned Caltex sites to rally around one key fundraising day. To help them, we leveraged local site marketing.

All Caltex sites were invited to opt-in to a local area marketing activation. This activation gave them access to point of sale (POS) material for their site and a banner that announced their fundraising efforts on Wish Drive Day. It also gave them the tools, information and support to run either a Gala Fundraising Day or a Driveway Service Day. Gala Days varied by site, but usually entailed activities such as a sausage sizzle and, sometimes, face-painting for children. Driveway Service Days offered motorists complimentary tyre checks and windscreen washes in return for a gold coin donation. Close to 400 Caltex sites got involved. It should be noted that these sites paid for the local area marketing tools and resources from their own budgets.

To communicate the Star Mart Wish Drive, Caltex invested in both radio and out-of-home advertising. The stores' forecourt POS was a key communication asset and the brand also leveraged all of its social media channels.

The business had agreed to provide some funding for the campaign but it wasn't a huge budget, so we had to dig deep to find opportunities to generate awareness of the campaign and the call to action.

Partnerships became a key amplification vehicle for the Star Mart Wish Drive message. These included partners that Caltex sponsored at the time such as Essendon Football Club, Subaru, Red Bull Racing and Triple Eight Race Engineering. These partners allowed Caltex to promote its message to the fans and members of those organisations. Racing driver, Craig Lowndes, with whom Caltex had a long-term partnership through its V8 sponsorship, rallied to the cause by telling his social media followers about the campaign and Caltex's partnership with Make-A-Wish. Lowndes also allowed Caltex to leverage his profile to amplify the message of the campaign.

No stone was left unturned on partnerships. The lift operator of Caltex's head office building donated media space for the campaign and the café on the ground floor also collected donations during the campaign period.

Local community days such as these are a very effective way of attracting new customer prospects from the local community.

Internal engagement for the Wish Drive Day was high. A morning tea was held to help fundraise and on Wish Drive Day, Caltex staff rallied around shaking donation tins on the street and helping out at Caltex sites.

It was a great success from a fundraising perspective. Over $400,000 in donations was raised for Make-A-Wish, which exceeded everyone's expectations. A hard goal hadn't been set in the first year, simply because there was no way of estimating the level of funds the campaign would raise.

Of all the fundraising sources, it was interesting to note that the local area marketing activation on Wish Drive Day generated the most funds. I know from my experience working with Caltex on local area marketing for 19 years that local community days such as these are a very effective way of attracting new customer prospects from the local community. They're equally effective in building a relationship between the store staff and their customers.

In 2014, the campaign rolled out with a slightly refreshed message. This time, over $420,000 was raised to help grant wishes for seriously ill children. Similarly, in 2015, the Star Mart Wish Drive raised over $500,000 for Make-A-Wish, bringing the total funds raised, across the three-year period, to over $1.3 million.

Caltex did not release commercial results for this campaign.

No doubt Caltex's focus is purely on the campaign's results in terms of fundraising and driving awareness of Make-A-Wish – an understandable position given the public's negative perceptions of the petrol retail category.

I'll go out on a limb, however, and say I would be surprised if Caltex didn't attract some positive commercial returns from this campaign, but that's simply my opinion.

FIVE TAKE-OUTS FROM CALTEX'S APPROACH TO CAUSE MARKETING

1. *Identify your assets.* Consider how you can structure a campaign around your key assets. (In Caltex's case, a massive store footprint was its major asset.)

2. *Money isn't everything.* If you have good assets, you may not need a large budget to support your cause marketing campaign.

3. *Leverage all your partner channels.* Partners are more likely to support you when there's a cause involved.

4. *Engage your staff.* Employees are willing to get active around a cause, especially when there is a big concerted, public effort that they can rally around.

5. *Annual campaigns can build over time.* Customer recognition means that to achieve similar levels of awareness year on year, you don't necessarily have to spend the same level of media budget for each campaign.

CHAPTER 17

AIRBNB

Until we all belong

In 2014, Airbnb introduced a new brand purpose. The company had started its repositioning work in 2013 as it tried to understand what Airbnb's role in the world was. To this end, the company interviewed hundreds of Airbnb employees, guests and hosts around the world and an insight emerged from the process. The last thing Airbnb guests want to be is tourists. They want to engage with people and culture, they want to be insiders. The idea of 'belonging' was seeded and by mid-2014, Airbnb had a new mission statement: to make people around the world feel like they could belong anywhere.

In February 2017, Airbnb backed up its mission in the most high-profile way. Following President Donald Trump's ban on refugees and immigrants from certain (mostly Muslim) nations, Airbnb ran a TVC titled *'#weaccept'* during the Super Bowl.

#weaccept doesn't mention Donald Trump or the travel ban but, instead, it focuses on the value of embracing differences. Still frames of close-up faces of people from diverse backgrounds

and race interchange while the overlaying text reads 'We believe no matter who you are, where you're from, who you love, or who you worship we all belong. The world is more beautiful the more you accept'.

Earlier, on behalf of the company, Airbnb's CEO Brian Chesky had offered free housing to refugees and anyone who was not allowed in the US. Airbnb backed the Super Bowl advertisement up with a statement that highlighted a goal to provide short-term housing to 100,000 'people in need' over the next five years. The statement went on to acknowledge 'the painful truth that guests on Airbnb have experienced discrimination, something that is the very opposite of our values. We know we have work to do and are dedicated to achieving greater acceptance in our community.'[1]

True to its purpose, Airbnb made a courageous stand on an issue that has been highly divisive. It doesn't take a genius to recognise that this stand would earn the company both supporters and detractors, perhaps in equal measures. Airbnb went ahead regardless, behaving like a true purpose-led brand.

Airbnb has also committed to contributing $4 million over four years to the International Rescue Committee to support the most critical needs of displaced populations globally.

Not surprisingly, Airbnb's #*weaccept* platform formed the basis of new terms of service that integrate non-discrimination rules for Airbnb hosts. In Australia, #*weaccept* became central to Airbnb Australia's activism on same-sex marriage.

Australia is one of the world's last major western democracies that does not recognise same-sex marriage. It's an extraordinary situation given the fact that a majority of Australians actually support marriage equality.

Airbnb in Australia has been a major partner of Sydney's Gay and Lesbian Mardi Gras since 2015. The company's support for the

LGBTQIA+ community was a reciprocation of the LGBTQIA+ community's early support and adoption of Airbnb.

In the lead up to the 2017 Mardi Gras parade, Airbnb launched a powerful and emotive initiative called 'Until We All Belong', which took a strong position of support for marriage equality in Australia. Through a TV advertising campaign, Australians were asked to pledge their support for marriage equality by wearing a specially crafted ring until same-sex marriage is recognised in our country.

The Airbnb campaign heralds a new era where businesses are answering the calls of consumers to get involved in solving some of society's greatest challenges.

Designer Marc Newson created the matte black ring with a unique feature, a gap in the middle, symbolising the gap in marriage equality. The words 'Until We All Belong' are engraved on its interior.

Instead of purely focusing on people from the LGBTQIA+ community, the advertisement features their families, loved ones and friends, a diverse range of people of all ages and backgrounds, describing the ring and what they believe it symbolises. It then shows the same people pledging to wear the ring until the people they love and care about can belong – my sister, son, uncle, cousin, mother, mate, brother, etc. The last words are left to those who are directly affected by marriage inequality with a final emotive statement – 'Until We All Belong'.

Those people wishing to take the pledge and get a ring are invited to visit the following website: www.untilweallbelong.com. Apart from postage costs, the ring was offered to people free of charge. Given the majority of the budget was needed to fund the production of the rings, this left Airbnb with a relatively low media budget.

As a result of this, partnerships became a strong force in getting the 'Until We All Belong' message seen and heard.

What is evident in this campaign is the unifying nature of a brand taking an important social stand. It heralds a new era where businesses are answering the calls of consumers to get involved in solving some of society's greatest challenges.

Here are just some of the businesses that partnered with Airbnb to unlock millions of dollars of media value through this campaign:

- *Qantas* was one of the highest profile supporters of this campaign, donating its media space and the backs of boarding passes to promote the cause
- *ANZ* communicated the message via its 1,500 ATMs nationally
- *ARN* offered radio program integration
- *Fairfax* provided digital banners and pre-roll advertising
- *oOH!* and *Pandora* radio each provided free media spots
- *Marie Claire* provided a six-page feature with celebrities
- *Google* offered up their top 25 YouTube influencers to raise awareness via their channels.

To get guidance on the cause itself, Airbnb partnered with Australian Marriage Equality (AME), an organisation that is working to achieve marriage equality in Australia. AME's Executive Director, Tiernan Brady, was previously the policy director of the Gay and Lesbian Equality Network (GLEN) – the organisation that is credited with success in achieving the 'yes' vote to marriage equality in Ireland.

At the time of writing (September 2017), 150,000 rings have been claimed.

A selection of comments from social media shows the depth of emotion felt by many people on the subject of marriage equality:

> Could do without that gap in marriage equality, Straya. Sort your shit out. *#untilweallbelong*

> As a wedding celebrant and a human, marriage equality is very close to my heart. I love this campaign and my new ring. *#untilweallbelong #loveislove*

> Proud to be rocking our new rings here. Well done @airbnb. *#equality #untilweallbelong*

> *#untilweallbelong*

> I have never felt so passionate about something, anyone who knows me or who I am would know my opinions on same sex love and equality. Today, I take the pledge to visually show my acceptance and beliefs on love. Whether it be same sex, different sex, you were born in the wrong body or you have no sexual preference, LOVE IS LOVE. How can we say we are a country of equality when so many judge on what love is?

> I'm wearing this incomplete ring alongside my wedding ring until it's possible for everyone to marry...

You may recall Australia's immigration minister, Peter Dutton, being very critical of the businesses taking a stand on this issue, telling Airbnb they should 'stick to their knitting'. What his statement suggests (and the subsequent statement of his colleague Eric Abetz), is that they're unaware of the public's strong desire for businesses to take a stand and to contribute to important social issues.

The irony here is that people are looking for strong positive leadership and, perhaps in the absence of this from their government representatives, the spotlight is now falling on businesses to pick up the slack. Businesses such as Airbnb are simply filling a void created by government inaction on issues that the public cares about.

FIVE KEY TAKE-OUTS FROM AIRBNB'S APPROACH TO CAUSE MARKETING

1. *Step up.* Brands are stepping into leadership positions on social issues, using the power of their marketing assets to drive awareness, invite collaboration and make a stand.

2. *Use cause marketing to bring your brand purpose to life.* It makes your purpose more authentic and believable.

3. *Use your assets.* Symbolism can be a powerful asset for purpose-led brands to drive engagement. In Airbnb's case, its #weaccept platform.

4. *Make it simple for the public to get involved.* People welcome the opportunity to collaborate.

5. *Join with like-minded organisations.* Cause-led activity can be a great unifying call for partners who will provide support and resources to optimise awareness and engagement.

---

1   Palazzo, Chiara, 2016, 'Airbnb host banned for denying transgender woman room after viral tweet', The Telegraph, available at: http://www.telegraph.co.uk/technology/2016/06/07/airbnb-host-banned-for-denying-transgender-woman-room-after-vira/

CHAPTER 18

ZAMBRERO

Mexican with a mission

My final example is an incredible Australian success story. It's a story that's less about cause marketing and more about purpose-led marketing and social entrepreneurship. This is a business with a social mission at its very heart, which is now a market leader and 12 years on from its launch it continues to enjoy strong growth and expansion.

Zambrero is the business I'm talking about and if you haven't heard about it yet, then keep your ears open because chances are you soon will, given the company's rate of expansion and its unique approach.

Let me first give you some context. Zambrero is a QSR franchise that sells fresh and healthy Mexican food to support humanitarian projects around the world and, more recently, in Australia. It has been recognised consistently as one of Australia's fastest growing franchises on the *BRW* Fastest Franchises list over recent years.

The mastermind behind Zambrero is Dr Sam Prince, a humanitarian, philanthropist, entrepreneur and medical doctor. He established his first restaurant in Braddon, Canberra when he was still a medical student at the age of 21. It was 2005 and his aim was to build a successful business that also helped people in need. It was his way of combining two of his desires outside of his medical career path – to help the underprivileged and to give expression to his entrepreneurial drive.

Since then, Dr Prince's vision has become a reality on a grand scale. As of May 2017, Zambrero has grown to over 150 restaurants in Australia. More recently, the business has established restaurants internationally in New Zealand, Ireland and Thailand and has plans to hit the US market in the future.

Most importantly, the humanitarian impact that was the founder's goal has been an unadulterated success.

At the heart of Zambrero's business is an initiative called Plate 4 Plate. For every burrito or bowl purchased, a meal is donated to someone in need in the developing world. Meals are donated via Rise Against Hunger (previously known as Stop Hunger Now), a hunger relief agency operating in developing countries, primarily distributing nutritious food through school feeding programs. Customers walking into Zambrero's restaurants are taken on a journey where they are met with the meal counter and graphics promoting the Plate 4 Plate initiative and highlighting Zambrero's tag line – Mexican with a mission.

In addition to the franchise restaurant business, Zambrero has also launched a retail range of grab and go products. For every product purchased from this range, a meal is donated to someone in an underprivileged Australian community. For this program, Zambrero partnered with Foodbank.

At the time of writing, over 15 million meals have been donated through these programs. No, that is not a typo – 15 million. If that doesn't impress you, try this for size – their goal is to reach 1 billion meals by 2025.

Similar to Patagonia (see Chapter 8), Zambrero doesn't stop at just one initiative, as powerful and impactful as it is as a standalone. The company also takes action to foster sustainability. The packaging used in Zambrero restaurants is made from recycled sugar cane pulp – a 100 per cent bio-compostable material which apparently disappears entirely in a home compost heap within 90 days. Even the staff t-shirts are made from recycled material.

Zambrero works hard to ensure that its product quality stands on its own merits, with food that is healthy, modern and fresh. The company also provides gluten-free, dairy-free and vegan options for all customers.

Zambrero staff are treated differently compared to other fast food companies. To encourage staff to pursue their purpose-seeking instincts, all employees receive five weeks of leave per year, instead of the usual four weeks, with the extra week spent visiting or investigating a humanitarian endeavour. I wonder how many future social entrepreneurs Zambrero is inspiring through this endeavour.

Another aspect of Zambrero's Plate 4 Plate initiative gives its customers hands-on active involvement. Plate 4 Plate meal packing days are held in different cities in Australia and they provide customers with the opportunity to volunteer their time to help pack meals for people in need. These meal packing days are oversubscribed and in 2016, volunteers packed over 350,000 meals.

The Zambrero team call their Plate 4 Plate initiative 'their very reason for being'. The sheer scale of the impact of this initiative is indisputable evidence of its success.

Now, as incredible as this story is, there's another story that has played out behind the scenes, that is less well known. Beyond the impact of the Plate 4 Plate initiative, Zambrero has underwritten the efforts of another entirely separate not-for-profit organisation.

One Disease is a non-profit organisation that was set up by Zambrero's founder, Dr Sam Prince, with the aim to eliminate disease from remote Indigenous communities. First on the hit list is crusted scabies – a devastating and highly contagious skin disease. If it is left untreated, 50 per cent of people with this disease could die within five years. One Disease is on track to eliminate crusted scabies from Australia by 2022. The One Disease crusted scabies elimination campaign will not only eliminate a serious disease, but it will also contribute to closing the gap and addressing Indigenous disadvantage in Australia.

When I interviewed Dr Sam Prince for this book, he initially questioned whether Zambrero belonged in the pages of a book on cause marketing. He highlighted that in the earlier years of the business Zambrero didn't even talk about or promote Plate 4 Plate, it was simply something it did. The initiative was never originally implemented with a view to market it for commercial gain.

In that respect, Sam is correct – it's not an example of cause marketing. There's a reason though that it does belong in this book. Zambrero is a shining example of how purpose can be at the heart of a successful for-profit venture. It's also a powerful example of how the profit derived from that venture can go even further to drive more social impact.

Cause marketing – where a business aligns with a cause or cause partner to create profit and social impact – can be a simple and effective *first step* for a business that wants to get its brand on the path to purpose. What Zambrero offers is the inspiration of just how far that brand can move along that path, if it chooses to.

SIX TAKE-OUTS FROM ZAMBRERO'S APPROACH TO CAUSE MARKETING

1. *Be unique.* A social purpose can provide a powerful point of difference to your competitors.

2. *Purpose attracts.* It not only attracts your customers, but staff and partners as well.

3. *Value your product.* Strong purpose-led brands still need to ensure their product stands on its own merits.

4. *Engage with the community.* Invite your customers to volunteer and collaborate with your brand.

5. *Build profit.* Zambrero is living proof that a purpose-led brand that contributes to a cause can also be highly profitable.

6. *Every journey starts with a first step.* The journey to purpose can start with cause marketing.

PART 3

A SIX-STEP METHODOLOGY TO CAUSE MARKETING

CHAPTER 19

SEVEN MISTAKEN BELIEFS

As I highlighted in the introduction of this book, if you're responsible for marketing a brand to consumers today, there's a good chance that you'll be working through at least one of the following problems, if not all three of them:

1. *Brand awareness and brand health.* Today's media-fractured environment means that you need a strategy that will cut through and seize the attention of consumers; one that goes beyond pricing and other tactical offers. The importance of building brand trust is also a priority for you.

2. *Short-term sales.* This focus on short-term sales is important but makes it incredibly hard to build a brand of substance, particularly if budgets are being cut year on year.

3. *Employee engagement.* Fast becoming recognised as a crucial part of the marketing mix, most CEOs and CMOs realise that a disengaged workforce will affect customer experience, making it increasingly harder to deliver a believable brand promise.

If these problems resonate with you, then you're probably already well aware of the value of brand purpose in tackling the first problem. You also probably realise that it's a big undertaking and there is no guarantee of success. It's a long-term strategy that won't generate the short-term sales that your team need to deliver. Besides all of that, you would need a big media budget, and how do you justify investment in a strategy that's unlikely to deliver immediate results?

If you're having some or all of these thoughts, you can take some solace in the fact that you're not alone. Many marketers are working through these same considerations. But there's an important piece in this thinking that is missing. Marketers need to think less about what their brand can say about itself in order to be relevant and start thinking more about what their brand can do for the world we live in.

Marketers need to think less about what their brand can say about itself in order to be relevant and start thinking more about what their brand can do for the world we live in.

There's a big difference. The former way of thinking is rooted in the 20th century advertising model, which involves an expectation that the consumer just sits there passively while marketers tell them about their brand. It amazes me how much of this still goes on. When was the last time, as a consumer, that you purchased a brand because of its advertising (unless it was for a special offer)? When was the last time you even clicked on a banner advertisement?

The latter approach – what a brand can contribute to the world authentically – offers an active opportunity to solve real-world problems that need solutions.

Which approach do you think is going to inspire people and create followers, supporters and collaborators who eagerly share your content?

Let's take a deeper dive. Those three major problems that I high-lighted usually stem from a lack of development in the following seven key areas.

1. The absence of a simple-to-implement strategic solution for building a more meaningful and purposeful brand

This common mistake is based on a misconception that purpose is exclusively about your brand positioning and what you say about your brand and how you communicate it. It entirely misses the opportunity that brands can start behaving with purpose by aligning with a cause (that has a credible association with their brand proposition) and taking action. Pampers 1 pack = 1 vaccine campaign (Chapter 6) started life as a simple Christmas promotion back in 2006 and continues as a world-changing program today. By aligning with UNICEF to take action to eradicate MNT, Pampers powerfully brings to life its brand positioning of caring for babies' happy, healthy development.

2. A lack of support and unity across the business about what your brand stands for

Without the buy-in and enthusiasm of your leadership team and the rest of the business, you're going to struggle to build a brand with depth and authenticity that people care about. A disengaged workforce will inevitably affect customer experience which makes delivering a believable brand promise a challenge. A big goal around a cause can inspire and unify your colleagues like little else can.

3. Lacking a realistic marketing solution that drives brand health and, simultaneously, unlocks short-term sales

Cause marketing can tackle both of these needs simultaneously but is rarely considered as a marketing solution because:

- it sits in the realm of corporate partnerships and is seen as a cost to the business; and

- there is a lack of awareness in Australia about its successful use as a strategic marketing platform.

4. An absence of collaboration opportunities for your consumers

Some of the world's best campaigns involve collaboration between the brand and its consumers. Airbnb Australia's #*until weallbelong* campaign (Chapter 17) for marriage equality is a great example of this and for good reason.

> *Consumers believe they could do more to support good causes by working together with brands. They also want brands to make it easier for them to make a positive difference.*[1]

Brands that recognise this are providing opportunities for consumers to be the heroes of their own stories. Through collaboration models, they're earning the attention and trust of consumers.

5. Lacking content that is personal, positive, inspiring and newsworthy

So much content is driven by price and promotion. That works fine from a tactical perspective, but it does nothing to build your brand in the hearts and minds of people. A cause or purpose-led marketing approach can unearth a treasure trove of stories, and we're not just talking stories about the beneficiaries of the cause. If you have a campaign or program with a good collaboration model, it can also stimulate people to tell and share their own stories of their experiences with the campaign or even your brand. Patagonia's Worn Wear campaign (Chapter 8) is a good example of a program that encourages people to share their own stories.

6. Not having a strategy to leverage all available assets

In today's media environment, marketers have to be smarter about how they communicate and look to non-traditional media channels. Partners, supporters, suppliers and other stakeholders all have assets that a business can leverage – databases, social media followers, physical assets, etc. You just need an inspiring reason for them to want to join forces with you and allow you to leverage their assets.

7. A lack of meaningful data to justify marketing investment in a purpose-led strategy

Metrics are the key to learning and optimising the performance of your marketing campaign or program. In the absence of meaningful metrics, you're going to struggle to make a strong business case for investment in a purpose-led marketing strategy. A cause marketing campaign can be a good starting point to establishing the commercial and social value of a purpose-led approach.

MY SIX-STEP SIMPLE METHODOLOGY

If you're relating to this, the good news is that there is a methodology that enables you to create a powerful cause marketing approach to build a more meaningful and purposeful brand.

It's a methodology I developed based on my own direct experience in cause marketing, as well as by deconstructing the critical success factors of some of the world's most successful cause and purpose-led marketing campaigns.

This methodology forms the framework for one of the product offerings my brand consultancy offers clients, the **Path to Purpose Program**. However, for those businesses that want to develop their cause marketing approach themselves, I'm pleased to be able to share the details of the framework in this chapter. Here's a quick overview before we take a deep dive into each of the modules.

When you know how, it really is SIMPLE.

1. Strategic foundations

A strong strategic foundation lays the groundwork for a cause partnership that is powerful, credible, authentic and clearly aligned with your brand positioning. This ensures you get full value out of all aspects of your program. It also gives you the basis of a purpose-led approach for your brand.

2. Internal alignment and engagement

Getting alignment and input from key stakeholders, including your leadership team, is an absolute necessity for a successful cause partnership. Ownership and belief in the partnership program is critical to adoption, which is why this part of the program centres on the establishment of an advisory and accountability cross-departmental team. This approach makes it easier for you to gain wider internal engagement and support from employees throughout the business.

3. Marketing activation plan

Build a marketing activation plan that delivers on your marketing objectives. Centre the marketing plan around three key brand metrics:

1. Brand engagement – participation, media impressions, social media impressions
2. Incremental sales increase
3. Brand health.

And three social metrics:

1. Social impact – fundraising and awareness
2. Delivery on your social purpose or social impact goal
3. Social return on investment (ROI).

Develop a clear marketing strategy, campaign concept and tactics to deliver on the above.

4. Public relations (PR) plan

PR is a vital piece of your cause marketing communication plan, particularly if you lack the budget to amplify your message effectively through TV, radio, print or outdoor advertising. The public relations plan comprises a five-step framework that ensures message clarity and relevance, targeted media placement and comprehensive media and ambassador management around launch events.

5. Leverage opportunities

A cause marketing campaign or program offers a unique opportunity that most generic brand campaigns don't – permission to leverage assets and resources of partner businesses for the greater good.

6. Evaluation

You should plan to optimise your cause marketing campaign or program over time. Metrics must be established and a reporting process agreed upon and implemented. Recommendations to improve and evolve the program should then be provided. Your impact communication plan will ensure all stakeholders are aware of the achievements of the campaign program from a brand and a social perspective. Being able to clearly report positive tangible results is also the crucial part for you to unlock ongoing investment into building a purpose-led brand.

---

1   Edelman Good Purpose Study: 71% of people believe brands and consumers could do more to support good causes by working together. 63% want brands to make it easier for them to make a positive difference.

CHAPTER 20

STRATEGY – THE FOUNDATIONS OF SUCCESS

A solid strategic foundation is one of the keys to success for your cause marketing campaign or program. This takes time and it's well worth ensuring you give yourself the time to get it right because if and when you're questioned on your choice of partner, you need to be able to prove the rigour you've applied to the process.

The following is a step-by-step process to working through strategy and assumes you're starting this process from scratch, you have no existing cause partner or, even if you do have an existing relationship, you're open minded to new partnership opportunities.

We start with some housekeeping points.

1. BUSINESS OR BRAND?

This is simple. Identify clearly whether this is a specific brand opportunity or whether you are looking at this as a business or masterbrand opportunity. Given that all of the examples I've shared with you are brand-led, there is clearly huge value for brands and this is by far the most common approach. Having said that, there are some good examples of a masterbrand or company-led approach such as Unilever's brightFuture project.

2. CAUSE OR PURPOSE?

Is this a cause marketing opportunity? Or are you in fact looking to develop a brand purpose? There is a world of difference in these two approaches. I've shared with you what I think is one of the best examples of a purpose-led brand, Patagonia. Purpose guides a brand's actions. It is about what the brand does, not what the brand says. It unifies your team, drives action, tells your story and defines your culture. It goes beyond the remit of the marketing team as it goes to the very heart of business transformation. For that reason, there are some complexities in developing a brand purpose. It's a subject worthy of a book in itself, so I'm not going to attempt to simplify it down to a couple of paragraphs in this section.

The purpose of this framework is to give you the tools to develop a successful cause marketing program or campaign. Cause marketing is a powerful way to bring an existing brand purpose to life. For brands that don't have a brand purpose, it offers them a path to purpose – a strong first step for their brand to behave with purpose and identify what it stands for.

3. COMPETITIVE REVIEW

Understanding what your competitors are doing in the area of cause, community or purpose-led marketing is an important early step. Most businesses communicate which not-for-profit (NFP) organisations they support and the programs that they're involved with on their website. Although it's important to know what your competitors are doing, just because they support a cause or organisation through CSR doesn't mean you can't support a similar cause or even the same cause. It will depend on the nature of their partnership.

Ultimately, if your competitors are quietly supporting a cause or NFP organisation, but not leveraging the partnership, then there is an open opportunity for you to align your brand with that cause if you feel it's the right area for your brand. If, however, your competitor is leveraging a partnership actively and developing awareness of the brand's association with and support for a cause, then there is little value in pursuing this course for your brand or business.

Now we start to drill into the meaty stuff.

4. SELECTING YOUR CAUSE

The single most important thing we look for in this process is a cause that is credible for your brand. Australian consumers can be cynical – maybe we're just realists, but a brand's association with a cause needs to pass the sniff test. For me, the most powerful partnerships are those where the cause is clearly aligned with the brand positioning.

For example, Pampers brand positioning is that it cares for babies' happy and healthy development. Pampers and UNICEF's one pack = one vaccine campaign targeted MNT and provided vaccines for at-risk babies and their mothers. This is a perfect alignment for the brand.

Allphones' partnership with Lifeline in 2015 was also an obvious match. Allphones is a mobile phone retailer and Lifeline's phone helpline service is underfunded and needs support. At the time, one in five calls to the Lifeline helpline went unanswered. The partnership with Allphones set out to generate much needed funding and awareness of Lifeline's services.

Another approach is to align the cause with something that affects your target audience or your employees. A great example of this is Hungry Jacks, which is a principal partner of R U OK?Day. Most of Hungry Jacks' 18,000+ staff are young people. We know that many young people today are struggling with self-esteem and confidence issues and are feeling increasingly disconnected. By partnering with R U OK?Day, Hungry Jacks is seeking to use its access to a large number of young people to good effect. The company is creating awareness of the importance of young people having meaningful conversations with their mates and Hungry Jacks is giving its staff the tools and encouragement to have those conversations.

A cause marketing approach can be a step on the path towards a brand identifying and developing an overarching brand purpose.

When considering which cause to align with your brand, it's important to also consider the following questions:

- Can your product itself be positioned as a solution for social improvement? (e.g. Dulux paint)
- Can your brand be an authentic champion of the cause? (e.g. ANZ's long-term support for Mardi Gras)
- Can you own this cause in the mind of consumers? (e.g. Cat saves cat).

It's so important to think first in terms of cause, rather than cause partner and not to feel limited to causes that have high profile partners. In fact, I would argue that the clearer you are on the cause and your intended social impact, the more credibility you build for your brand with your stakeholders.

This stance has another very strong benefit. When you think first about which cause partner to align your brand with, the first thing that most marketers will jump on is the fundraising opportunity. How can we raise the maximum funds for the NFP partner? There's no question that there's value in that, but the real opportunity is in becoming invested in the cause itself. What impact can you help to deliver by involving your brand? What assets do you have to help you achieve that impact? How else can you contribute positively to the cause?

REI's #OptOutside campaign demonstrates brilliantly what you can achieve when you think this way. By thinking first about the cause, they created a campaign that was far more powerful than a fundraising platform for some environmental group. They created a movement.

5. CAUSE PARTNER RESEARCH

Once you have clarity on what kind of cause you want to be aligned with, you can start looking at partners. Nothing really beats good old-fashioned online research here. However, there are also a few resources here to help you:

- Pro Bono Australia has a guide to giving (a directory of charities and NFP organisations) that is available on its website.
- The Australian government's Australian Charities and Not-for-profits Commission (ACNC) has a register containing information on more than 54,000 charities.

Once you've identified the organisations operating in the targeted cause area, have a good look at what each of them does, noting their differences and the programs they invest in. I find it useful at this stage to get this information up on a whiteboard so you can clearly see the areas that your brand may be able to impact.

Make sure you also check their existing sponsors and any who may be your competitors.

I would then narrow the contenders down to five or six organisations that I think have the best fit for my brand, assuming that there are that many NFP organisations working in that cause area.

6. EVALUATION CRITERIA AND ANALYSIS

Up to this point, we've taken an expansive view of the potential partners. Now, we start to narrow down. Sometimes it's tempting to just zero in on the NFP organisations that we know well. You can do this but, in my experience, there's value in going through this process as it can highlight some interesting opportunities.

The process for establishing your criteria is a combination of getting input from your fellow employees and through workshopping your ideas. I strongly recommend *against* asking your fellow employees what cause they would like the brand or business to support. That question is highly subjective and, in many cases, deeply personal. You're rarely going to get everyone to agree and, in the worst-case scenario, it can create division and anger. I know this from personal experience.

In my previous business, I had about 20 employees. I wanted our business to support a cause and I thought, rather than me autocratically choosing the cause and partner, I would put it to a vote. I invited all of my employees to put up their chosen cause. We had a meeting with the whole team and everyone who wanted to submit their cause was given five to ten minutes to talk about it. At the end of the process, we all voted.

It all started so well. I saw people get up and talk with such incredible passion. Some of these were people who had never given a presentation in their lives and never wanted to, until now.

It was amazing. That is, until the votes came in and then all hell broke loose.

I was shocked at how upset some people were. An animal charity had the most votes and some people couldn't get their heads around that, saying to me 'how can they put an animal's life ahead of a human being's life?' It caused so much division and unhappiness because these were causes that people felt passionately about. Ultimately, we ended up supporting three organisations to try to satisfy everybody. It's not a process I'll go through again. It certainly taught me how *not* to choose a cause partner.

Internal input

So, what kind of input do we want to get from employees? We don't want to ask which causes they support. Rather, we want to know what things they consider to be important when selecting a cause partner. I think a ranking process is useful here – something you can do easily via an online survey.

Here are some options that you could include in your survey to prompt your employees when considering which type of cause they would like to see the brand support:

- Large, well-known charity
- Small, lesser known charity for whom we can have a major impact
- Volunteering opportunities
- Fundraising opportunities
- Product donation opportunities
- Australian charity, local impact
- Global charity, global impact
- Global charity, Australian impact
- Credible association – i.e. relevant to our business or to our customers
- Other (please provide details).

These are just some ideas and you will need to think about this from the perspective of your own business. Once you get the results back, evaluate the most valued criteria based on everyone's combined responses.

Criteria workshop

Now it's time to get your team together. Ideally, your team should involve people from marketing, the CSR or corporate citizenship department and human resources (HR).

With your team, simply brainstorm what you all deem to be the most important criteria for this partnership. Initially go for quantity over quality – listing as many things that people feel are important on a whiteboard. Apart from all of the prompters above, you might also want to consider some of the following criteria as you start to consider the marketability of the partnership:

- Partner profile
- National presence
- Local grassroots profile
- High profile or celebrity patrons/supporters
- Program specific opportunities
- Tangible impact outputs (e.g. Pampers one pack = one vaccine).

Once you've got everything written down, including the most valued things as highlighted by your survey, ask the workshop attendees to write down their five most important criteria. There is likely to be overlap and you should start to see a clear picture forming of what criteria is most important to the business. Before you lock in your key criteria (which ideally shouldn't be more than six), you should do a sense check on it.

Evaluation analysis workshop

This is where you take your five or six NFP partners, along with the information on their focus, programs, etc., and evaluate them against the key criteria that you've selected from your workshop. It's a good idea to use the same team of people during this workshop as you did for the previous exercise.

Give each criteria a score. If all criteria are seen as equally important, give them all a score out of 10. If any are considered more important, weight the scoring towards the more important criteria. Then, as a group, evaluate the score of each NFP partner against each of the criteria from zero to 10 with '10' being the best fit.

You should end up with a clear picture of which NFP partner is your ideal fit based on the agreed criteria. Having said that, I recommend shortlisting the top two partners and reaching out to both. There may also be other factors that come into your final selection of partner, including which organisation you feel you could work best with.

7. PARTNER SELECTION

Be aware that NFP organisations don't have the same resources as for-profit businesses. For this reason, it's important that while you're doing your due diligence you do it in a way that respects the NFP organisation's time. Also be mindful that some business categories can pose problems for some NFP organisations. For example, alcohol is a brand category that some NFP organisations simply cannot partner with.

Perhaps consider an initial approach by phone and follow up with an email with any questions you may have. All being well, go to the next step of holding a meeting with the NFP organisation and learn what you need to about the work it does, the programs it supports and what its needs are. Drilling into the organisation's needs and where its funds are most needed can give you valuable insights about the role your brand or business and its stakeholders can play.

Give the NFP organisation as much visibility as you can on how you are looking to leverage the partnership and what you will need from them. This is definitely a conversation to have upfront to manage expectations from the get-go and avoid any unwelcome surprises. Timings are an important subject to discuss as is process. As guardians of their brand, an NFP partner will naturally want to see any communications that feature their brand. The organisations will need to be part of the creative approval process. Find out upfront how quickly the NFP partner is able to provide approvals. If you have a short lead-time and the partner has long approval timings, it might be a deal breaker. It is better for all parties to know this straight away. If you can identify a potential problem during this negotiation period, you may be able to work together to find ways to circumvent it.

Drilling into the organisation's needs and where its funds are most needed can give you valuable insights about the role your brand or business and its stakeholders can play.

The other important conversation to have is regarding the length of the partnership. You need to consider whether this partnership is going to be a one-off or a commitment to a long-term partnership over a few years.

From an authenticity perspective, I believe long-term partnerships deliver more for everyone and there are many case studies to back this up. There is a lot of value to the commercial brand in having a partnership program that offers a recurring annual marketing campaign. That said, you may not be in a position to sign a two- or three-year agreement, in which case you'll need to make it a one-year agreement with an option to renew.

8. SIGNING A MEMORANDUM OF UNDERSTANDING (MOU)

Once both parties are in agreement to go ahead with the partnership, you'll need to sign a memorandum of understanding (MOU). This is essentially 'an agreement to agree' or an agreement to enter into a more specific and comprehensive contract or agreement at a later time after further negotiations and when you both have more clarity around the specifics of the agreement.

Even though the MOU is not normally a legally binding document, this is the time to get your legal department involved. The MOU usually sets out the framework for the collaboration of both parties and expresses the common goals of each of the parties to the agreement.

9. SOCIAL IMPACT

While the MOU is being drafted, you can get to work on identifying exactly where you want your impact to be directed and what kind of impact you're targeting. Is there a particular program you want to support? If so, what impact could you achieve over a specified period of time? If it's general fundraising, have a think about what level of funds you could potentially raise. Ask your NFP partner what those funds will be able to achieve.

I think it makes a world of difference if you can see beyond dollars and, instead, focus on the impact of those dollars. It's about thinking transformationally rather than transactionally. The difference it can have in how you approach and communicate your cause marketing campaign can be immense. It becomes so much more personal and it opens the door to sharing stories. It's those stories that will connect with your people internally as well as your customers and other stakeholders.

In the first year of your partnership, it might be difficult to assess what level of impact or fundraising you can achieve but I recommend you start with a big hairy audacious goal (BHAG). You don't need to commit to this goal but put it out there for your team to think about and, for goodness sake, don't be conservative. The bigger the goal, the bigger the scale of ideas to get there!

10. SOCIAL PURPOSE

By now you should have clarity on what your targeted impact is going to be and where or how it will be delivered. I believe there is real value in taking another step and asking yourself what social purpose your brand serves. This will define your brand's higher purpose. If you get it right, it can unlock all kinds of other thinking around the brand that might otherwise be untapped.

Dove is a great, well-known example of a brand with a social purpose. Dove's social purpose is its brand purpose: to help women reconsider and redefine what real beauty is.

Clarifying your brand's social purpose takes it into brand-purpose territory. Whether you choose to communicate that purpose immediately or wait to build some momentum will be determined by the strategy you create.

CHAPTER 21

INTERNAL ALIGNMENT AND ENGAGEMENT

There is something quite unique about a cause marketing campaign. Unlike anything else, it creates an opportunity to unify a business across separate and often siloed divisions. With the right approach and a cause that is well aligned to your brand, the benefits of a cause marketing campaign can be felt across the business.

There are three fundamental factors that will set up your cause marketing program for success:

1. CEO alignment and support;
2. having a cross-departmental advisory and accountability team; and
3. establishing a big and unifying vision that the whole business can get behind and that inspires and energises the company's employees.

1. CEO ALIGNMENT AND SUPPORT

Over the last few years I and members of my team have attended the Cause Marketing Forum Conference (now called Engage for Good). We've attended talks and discussion groups about the world's most successful cause marketing campaigns. We've also been immersed in the subject of cause marketing and observed the successful, the almost successful and the also rans.

A consistent picture arises among the programs that have achieved optimal success. The corporate organisations involved had the alignment and support of the CEO early in the development of the partnership. While that support may be largely symbolic, the CEO's support for a project – particularly a project with a vision or goal attached to it – has a way of igniting action across divisions.

Back in 2012, one of the successful programs being showcased at the global conference was Coca-Cola's support of World Wildlife Fund's (WWF) Arctic Home program. This program ran in the US and Canada and saw Coca-Cola raising awareness of the plight of the polar bear, an icon that the brand had been associated with through its advertising for decades. Arctic Home was a phenomenal campaign and a massive investment. Coca-Cola changed all of its packaging, including turning their iconic red cans white as part of the Arctic Home campaign.

During the session on this campaign, one of the speakers who was part of the marketing team from Coca-Cola highlighted the CEO factor as a vitally important part of the success of the campaign. She said that Coca-Cola's CEO was invited on a trip to the Arctic by their NFP partner, WWF. The CEO, Muhtar Kent, was in the enviable position of being able to see real polar bears, upfront and close – it was a breathtaking experience. During his trip, Kent also learnt that climate change is causing the ice to melt and the natural habitat of polar bears is under threat. It was clear that without action, time was running out for polar bears.

This must have been an incredibly emotional experience for him. According to the Coca-Cola speaker at the conference, the CEO's support of the campaign was personal. We don't know how much that impacted the sheer scale and audacity of the Coca-Cola campaign, but my take-out from the speaker was that it counted for a lot.

If you're not familiar with the Arctic Home campaign, it is well worth seeking out. As part of Coca-Cola's partnership with WWF, the goal was to raise funds to create a 'last ice area' – a sustainably managed and preserved area of ice for polar bears, indigenous communities and commercial activities.

To help achieve this goal, Coca-Cola committed $2 million in funds over five years and pledged to match up to a further $1 million in donations made by their consumers via texting package codes in the first year of activation. In its first year, Coca-Cola raised $1.8 million through the packaging initiative. Added to the first year down payment of $400,000, year one of the campaign was deemed a fundraising success with $2.2 million going to the WWF program. That isn't to mention the impact the campaign also had in raising awareness of the plight of the polar bear.

In Coca-Cola's own words back in 2012, this was the biggest investment in a marketing campaign that the company had ever made. It was a runaway success. Here are the results on the 2012 campaign as a whole:

Social value:

- $1.8 million in donations (in the US and Canada)
- Coca-Cola paid its first instalment of its five-year commitment of $2 million to WWF

- In its first year, the campaign totalled over $2 million –
a significant contribution towards WWF's $10 million goal
- Awareness of the polar bear issue increased from 38 per
cent to 52 per cent.

Commercial results for Coca-Cola:

- 0.6 per cent lift in market share (considering the category,
a significant uplift)
- Growth in brand awareness 1.0 points
- 85 customers (trade accounts) activated the program
- 9 per cent increase in displays
- 380 million earned impressions on top of 1.4 billion paid
impressions
- 3.1 million website visits.

2. CROSS-DEPARTMENTAL ADVISORY AND ACCOUNTABILITY TEAM

I've written about the benefits of a good cause marketing program being felt right across the business. For that reason, I believe it's important for key stakeholders across the business to be responsible for the success of the partnership.

Recently, I met with one such team from a well-known luxury car brand. The brand had recently instigated a new partnership with an NFP partner and had appointed a team of individuals from different departments to be accountable for the success of the partnership program. What impressed me was that most of the team were heads of their departments or some of the most senior people in their departments. I'm not denigrating the efforts or impact of less senior people. The reason I was impressed was that it showed a commitment by the business and reflected the importance that it placed on the partnership opportunity for the business as a whole.

There is significant value in having an advisory and accountability team with representatives from across all business divisions. It opens up the opportunity to optimise the partnership program. Each department representative can highlight opportunities to leverage and amplify the partnership. Representatives can also identify potential challenges, which the group can then work out how to overcome together.

Regular meetings (the frequency of which will be determined by both the timing of the planned partnership activation and the availability of the group) will keep plans moving forward, with responsibilities, actions and deadlines agreed at the end of each meeting.

Once a full plan is developed, it should be approved by this group. The group should also review the activity and results and agree how best to refine and move forward. I'm not suggesting the whole partnership program should be run by the group. There needs to be an individual or a core team who has ultimate responsibility. However, the advisory and accountability team should be accountable for the involvement of their departments.

3. UNIFYING VISION

During the strategy development stage, you will have identified what social impact the business was looking to create and you may have gone a step further to develop a social purpose for your brand.

This is the piece that will unify people in action. Sure, it can be about fundraising and targeting a dollar amount. However, there is incredible power in drilling down to the raw benefits of what those funds will deliver.

Zambrero has a truly audacious goal – one billion meals funded through its Plate 4 Plate program by 2025. The company has documented this goal and you can be certain that it inhabits the minds of most of its people, from the business leaders to the frontline staff.

Virgin Mobile's #mealforameal campaign, for example, set a huge target of 400,000 meals to be funded by people snapping and sharing a photograph of their meals. In the first year alone, over a quarter of a million people shared their meals on social media and Virgin Mobile funded 260,000 meals through OzHarvest as a result.

In the second year of the partnership, both parties were still fixated on the original target and for that reason they widened the lens of the activation, inviting people to share all meals, good and bad, not just the beautiful ones.

The big target influenced Virgin Mobile's employees' behaviour. Many of the staff used their entitlement of one paid day per year to volunteer with OzHarvest, preparing and delivering meals for people and families in need.

Pampers' one pack = one vaccine campaign is a beautiful example of the power of a unified vision. The brand's vision – all the way back to the early days of the campaign – was to eliminate MNT from the globe. Ten years later, Pampers is so much closer to achieving that goal and is continuing with its campaign.

Not only is this an external marketing campaign, there is an internal employee engagement program attached to this program. The results of the internal program are perhaps just as important as the consumer-facing campaign. Employees of P&G, Pampers' parent company, are able to volunteer to be involved in the program which includes visiting the countries that are the recipients

There is significant value in having an advisory and accountability team with representatives from across all business divisions.

of the MNT vaccination program and assisting in the on-the-ground support of the program's work.

Apparently there was a huge waiting list for the volunteer program and the Pampers' business unit now posts among the company's highest rates of employee satisfaction.

Additionally, an employee engagement program was also designed to offer the company's NFP partner, UNICEF, some real benefits. P&G employees from offices in different countries could apply for a stint where they could train UNICEF in marketing communications or other expertise.

All of this was driven by a massive vision to eliminate MNT from the face of the globe. It was a rallying call that unified P&G employees across divisions within the business and around the world.

CHAPTER 22

MARKETING ACTIVATION PLAN

Create your big idea

The marketing aspect of cause marketing is the part I get insanely excited about. There are a couple of reasons for this. The first is that the majority of marketers in Australia simply aren't aware of the power of cause marketing to solve some of their very real and pressing problems. As marketers, we often wonder:

- How do I get my target audience to emotionally connect with my brand?
- How do I generate incremental sales?
- How do I get my franchisees motivated and energised?
- How do I get support from my trade partners?
- How do I support my social media channels?
- How do I get the business to support our marketing efforts and collaborate to amplify our marketing communication?

If you read some of the case studies from Part 2, you'll know I'm not talking out of my hat when I highlight cause marketing as a solution to these problems. Those example campaigns are the tip of the iceberg. There are many examples of cause marketing campaigns and programs that solve these challenges and deliver social impact and business success.

The second reason is this: it is the win-win-win (brand-cause-consumer) aspect of cause marketing that has the power to change the world. It also has the power to change how we market. Imagine brands as educators and champions for social change. Understand that and you grasp the sheer scale of the opportunity.

Following are some guidelines to help you develop an effective cause marketing approach for your brand. Getting started is usually the hardest part. Where do you start? Well, if you've done due diligence on your strategy, then it won't be as hard as you think. The following 10 tips will help guide you through this process.

1. BRAND PARTNERSHIPS MUST BE CREDIBLE

I've talked at length about this point but it's important to raise it again in this section. You hopefully have a cause and a partnership that is aligned with your brand or business. Now you've got to ensure that this alignment and credibility comes through clearly in your marketing.

Some partnership alignments may be more obvious than others. The key here is to make it easy for your customer to see the credible connection between your brand and the cause partner.

Airbnb's support for marriage equality, 'Until We All Belong', was a direct expression of the brand's purpose – 'To make people around the world feel like they could "belong anywhere."'

If you're familiar with the brand's mission statement, then this cause campaign makes absolute sense and is a perfect alignment for the brand. But what about people who might not be so familiar with Airbnb?

Airbnb ensured that it closed that loop. The campaign was called 'Until We All Belong'. The brand reinforced its mission through all communications, highlighting that acceptance and belonging are at the heart of Airbnb and that focus has brought its attention to the LGBTQIA+ community and the support needed for marriage equality in Australia.

This communication approach ensures Airbnb's support for marriage equality is credible, regardless of how familiar people are with the brand and what it stands for.

2. START WITH YOUR BRAND'S SOCIAL PURPOSE

A real commitment to make a difference lies at the heart of the most successful campaigns. Go back to your brand's social purpose and articulate it. If you're not clear on it, now's the time to be clear. When your social purpose leads your approach, it's actually quite amazing how well it will drive your marketing solutions.

Make your commitment to make a difference the foundation of your plan and you'll find so much will flow from it. Let's look at some examples of this.

Note: I've made some assumptions and have done a bit of reverse-engineering in order to illustrate this.

ANZ GAYTMs and GAYNZ

Social purpose (assumed):
• ANZ will contribute to and be a proud supporter of a culture of diversity and inclusion.

Marketing strategy:
• A celebration of LGBTQIA+ culture.

Execution:
• GAYTMs – Give ATMs a personality makeover. Each ATM will highlight a different over-the-top fashion style of the LGBTQIA+ community.

- GAYNZ – Turn the Oxford Street branch into a fantasy wonderland of LGBTQIA+ culture.

Pampers and UNICEF's one pack = one vaccine campaign

Social purpose:
- Eliminate MNT from the globe.

Marketing strategy:
- Awareness and fundraising
- Use marketing assets to drive awareness of the partnership through packaging, POS, TVC, PR, online, etc.
- Make the consumer the hero – have a transactional mechanic with every purchase.

Execution:
- One pack = one vaccine

Virgin Mobile – Making Mobile Better

Social purpose:
- Change the game for good.

Marketing strategy:
- Look at mobile behaviour and turn it into a positive action.

Execution:
- #mealforameal – snap and share a photo of your meal and Virgin Mobile will donate to OzHarvest to fund a meal for someone in need.
- R U OK?Day conversation partner – offering free calls for people to call a friend on R U OK?Day.

3. GO BEYOND COMMUNICATING YOUR PARTNERSHIP

Don't limit your marketing to a simple and passive promotion of the partnership between your brand and your cause partner.

Instead, think about how you can engage your customer or consumer in your cause activity. Think about your brand as an activist for the cause and ask yourself how it would behave. As I've said before, don't be fearful about your brand being seen to profit out of the partnership. If you have a credible and authentic partnership and you are committed for the right reasons, it is entirely proper and reasonable and acceptable for your brand to do well as a result of doing good.

The most successful partnerships are the ones that activate every channel and opportunity to drive impact. It's no coincidence that Pampers' one pack = one vaccine stands proudly as one of P&G's most successful marketing programs ever and that it has led the eradication of MNT from the globe. In true P&G style, the company has leveraged and amplified this campaign through every possible channel available. Pampers looks and behaves like a brand that is fully invested in achieving the social impact of eliminating MNT from the globe.

4. THINK BIG

What impact could you achieve if your business threw its full energy into this? Establish a BHAG (big hairy audacious goal). You can always come back from this. The point is to change the way you think about your partnership. Whatever you think you can achieve, double it. Now, look around at how you're going to achieve that.

Pampers' big goal is, indeed, audacious. It is to eliminate MNT from the planet. It doesn't get much bigger than that.

5. LEVERAGE YOUR ASSETS (ALL OF THEM)

Identify all the assets you have that you can use as part of your drive towards your social purpose. Highlight the assets you think will be the most value to you in achieving your social purpose.

Your own product is a key asset here, whether it's a packaged product or a retail network or an online website. Think about your assets and think of every touchpoint you have at your disposal with your customer.

When we were developing the Star Mart Wish Drive for Caltex, we recognised the biggest asset that Caltex had was its store footprint. Millions of people visit a Caltex store every month. Knowing that people want brands to make it easy for them to do good, it was an easy conclusion to come to – to use Caltex sites as a fundraising hub for Make-A-Wish.

6. MAKE YOUR CUSTOMER THE HERO

How can you enable your consumer or customer to be the hero? It doesn't just have to be your brand that contributes to the cause. People want brands to make it easier for them to do good. So how can you make it easy for your customers to contribute in some way to your cause or social purpose?

Shake Shack's Great American Shake Sale does this simply and effectively. Shake Shack invites its customers to donate in-store and, in return, the company gives their customers a voucher for a free shake to redeem on their next visit. It's a lovely way to thank the customer for their actions and, by the way, it's a great incentive to those customers to come back to Shake Shack to redeem the voucher.

7. SMALL WORKS BETTER THAN BIG

Have you ever seen an advertisement for a charity where the sheer scale of the problem seems overwhelming? One of the big foreign aid organisations ran advertisements like that 10 or 15 years ago. As a viewer, you felt so disempowered that it was difficult to watch. That is known as the 'collapse of compassion', which is defined as:

'As the number of people in need of help increases, the degree of compassion people feel for them ironically tends to decrease.'[1]

That is why small works better than big, e.g. adopt a child, buy a goat for a village, one pack = one vaccine, plate4plate.

All of these are tangible effects that empower people to act to create impact. If you can find a way to drill into a tangible benefit like this, that is a win. Be careful that you don't get caught up in something that ends up feeling contrived.

8. USE STORYTELLING TO BRING YOUR CAMPAIGN TO LIFE

Supporting a cause unlocks a wonderful opportunity to emotively connect with your customer. With every cause, there are compelling stories to tell. However, always remember that you are inviting your customer to join you on a journey of hope, so make sure the stories you tell reflect that.

You can tell your stories through the medium of film or television, via a TVC. Online videos make great shareable content. Of course, print advertisements are made for storytelling. Even POS can tell a visual story by providing a caption for context.

Coca-Cola used storytelling beautifully for its Arctic Home campaign a few years ago. To bring the campaign to life, Coca-Cola collaborated with *To the Arctic 3D* IMAX® filmmakers. They used footage from the film in Coca-Cola's TVC, featuring a mother and baby polar bear. The effect was an exquisite high quality, movie-style advertisement that was both beautiful and emotive.

9. STRESS TEST YOUR EXECUTION

When a brand is involved with a cause, it invites an emotive response from its customers and the market. The brand has to tread carefully. It has to be sensitive to the emotional responses it might generate or even the offence it may cause. If it's seen to overstate its support, the response can be negative. If it's seen as being opportunistic, for example by profiting out of a crisis, the response from the market can be swift and deadly.

The example of Bing Lee back in 2011 stands out in my mind here. Bing Lee offered to donate $1 to the Queensland flood donation appeal for every 'like' it gained on Facebook. This social media drive drew immediate backlash with many Twitter users criticising the retailer's attempt to capitalise on the floods and some using the hashtag #*charityfail*.

It is absolutely *critical* that you stress test your execution – your proposition, your call to action, your tone and the role you cast the brand in for this value exchange. Unless you have a brand that trades on polarising the market, I recommend you tread the sensitive path. Just like any other marketing campaign, execution can let down what might otherwise be a sound strategy.

Starbucks #racetogether

One campaign that became known for the wrong reasons was Starbucks #racetogether – an initiative that was launched in the US market.

Starbucks' founder, Howard Schultz, is well-known for pushing boundaries and trying different things. He has a well-documented philosophy that corporations have obligations to society beyond what tangibly impacts their bottom lines. With 22,000 stores and 75 million customers each week, Starbucks has immense power to influence social issues and public debate.

Starbucks #racetogether was a campaign designed to provoke a national conversation on race. The campaign involved Starbucks baristas writing '#racetogether' on coffee cups, which was designed to get them talking to customers about racial tension.

Customers did not respond well to the initiative. Critics branded it as insensitive and tone deaf and social media was awash with criticism. Some people felt that race was an uncomfortable issue to bring up and Starbucks was not an appropriate venue to talk about race. Others believed the campaign felt superficial for an issue of such depth. The campaign did provoke a national conversation, but not the kind of conversation that Starbucks was hoping for.

Despite the failure of the campaign, some commentators have praised the company for having the courage to try to tackle big issues. As for the CEO's response, Howard Schultz responded in an interview with *Fast Company* saying, 'We made a tactical mistake. So what? We're moving forward'.

For a powerful company such as Starbucks, the brand might be able to shrug off a tactical fail like that because of the credibility it has built up in taking a strong social stand on issues. For most other businesses, that luxury doesn't exist.

My advice is to take the sensitivity stress test. Test your execution among a broad range of people and then ask yourself what your grandmother would say about the campaign. Err on the side of caution unless, of course, you want to stir up the marketplace. In that situation, you have a different set of criteria to apply.

10. REPORT BACK ON YOUR RESULTS AND RECOGNISE YOUR CUSTOMERS' EFFORTS

When the campaign is over for the year and the results are in, you have an open opportunity to re-engage with your customers. Whether you set a goal for the campaign, for the year or even a longer-term goal, people will want to know the results. So, tell them.

This is the kind of information that social media is tailormade for. You're telling your followers about actions your brand has taken in collaboration with them. Tell them the results, tell them anecdotes and stories from the campaign trail, share photographs and, most importantly, thank them for their involvement. Hero their efforts and recognise them. Invite them to share their stories as well. This is a human effort and it's such a wonderful opportunity to show a human side of a business, so use the opportunity well.

Use those 10 tips as a filter and you'll find new ways of looking at your campaign opportunity.

---

1   https://thoughtsofascent.wordpress.com/2015/02/07/the-collapse-of-compassion/

CHAPTER 23

PUBLIC RELATIONS

Amplify your message

Once you've finalised your marketing activation plan, it's time to start thinking about public relations (PR). If you don't have a media budget, or if your media spend is minimal, PR is a vital piece of your cause marketing communication plan.

My advice is to not succumb to a desire to minimise costs at this stage. Use a PR professional. If you don't have an existing PR agency, invest in one or work with a PR consultant. Their skills and network will ultimately save you time and money and will give you the best opportunity to get your message heard in the media.

Also avoid the idea of using your cause partner's PR function. I speak from experience on this point. There's no doubt that media partners are quite partial to media alerts from NFP organisations. The downside is that there will be a reluctance to promote the for-profit partner. The value of getting great media for your cause marketing campaign will quickly disappear if your brand isn't even mentioned.

A good PR professional will be able to smoothly navigate the sensitivities that go hand-in-hand with cause marketing. A PR professional will also be able to strategise your social media plan to support your program or campaign. It's important to get PR involved in your campaign upfront, ideally at the strategy stage. A PR professional will be viewing a cause partnership through a different set of eyes – that of the media. It's hugely valuable to have this perspective upfront.

A good PR professional will be able to smoothly navigate the sensitivities that go hand-in-hand with cause marketing.

We partner with Social Mission, a PR consultancy that specialises in cause marketing. Their five-step process ensures message clarity and relevance, targeted media placement and comprehensive media and ambassador management around launch events.

SOCIAL MISSION'S FIVE-STEP PR PROCESS

1. *Media kit creation*

   This includes interviews with your CEO (or other senior representatives of your business) and an interview with the NFP, along with biographies and high resolution images of each.

   Key message soundbites are created at this stage, as well as more detailed information about the nature of the partnership, including common goals and activities.

2. *Target audience and key media identification*

   This stage involves identifying key media and influencers to reach your target audience and the creation of customised pitches for each targeted publication.

3. *Pitch to media*

This is where the value of your PR professional's network comes into its own. Your campaign is one of hundreds that are fighting for media support. You want to ensure yours has the best opportunity to reach its mark.

4. *Leverage ambassadors*

Celebrity ambassadors can be valuable assets to a cause campaign. Celebrities are also often more supportive of cause campaigns than campaigns that are for purely commercial purposes.

Lending celebrities' star power can be a powerful way to engage their supporters and the wider community in your campaign. Take a strategic approach to this and you'll get a much bigger bang for your buck than if it's an after-thought.

5. *Media management for on-the-day launch event*

If your cause campaign involves an event of any kind, this represents a great opportunity to engage the media. This is something that needs considered planning. You'll need to create a media list, pitch story angles to the media, pitch the event itself and manage any invitations.

CHAPTER 24

LEVERAGE YOUR PARTNERSHIPS

When I talk about leveraging partnerships, I'm talking about your cause partner plus every other potential partner you can bring to the table to contribute to or participate in your cause marketing program.

Let's start with your cause partner.

Your leverage opportunities with your cause partner will depend on the nature of your partnership and the level of support or sponsorship you have committed to them.

It's good to understand your partner's perspective. The organisation will have equity in its brand. You're partnering with them and leveraging their brand because of the emotional value and the recognition of the brand.

You might want to discuss possible amplification opportunities with your partner around the following assets:

1. *The organisation's website.* Apart from being featured as one of the organisation's supporting partners, during the

campaign period it is valuable to promote the campaign on the home page of their website if your partner is open to doing so. It is a good way to drive awareness of the campaign to the organisation's supporters.

2. *EDMs to their database.* One of the biggest assets for an NFP organisation is their loyal supporters. Don't be too surprised if the organisation is reluctant to use this channel to promote your offer – some will and some won't. The reason for this is simply to protect their most loyal supporters from being bombarded with messages. It is worth having a conversation around this and understanding if the NFP is comfortable allowing you to get your message across to its supporters.

3. *Newsletters to their support base.* It's quite common for NFPs to have newsletters that are sent out to their supporters and other stakeholders, telling them about news and events. This is a great vehicle to highlight your campaign and tell their supporters how they can support the partnership and optimise fundraising opportunities. Being a newsletter, it is considered less intrusive than an EDM to the NFP's supporter base.

4. *Other events.* Do your research and find out what other events your NFP partner is involved in. It may be another channel for you to promote your campaign.

5. *Other partners and sponsors of your cause partner.* Look at which other brands are involved with the cause. There might be collaboration opportunities or cross-company amplification opportunities.

   Airbnb leveraged partnerships very strongly when bringing 'Until We All Belong' to life. Partner leverage was a key component in driving awareness, with millions of dollars in media value delivered.

6. *Email signatures.* Creating a campaign email signature for your company is something you should look at being displayed during the promotional period. It's also an opportunity to ask your NFP partner to display the same or a similar signature.

You might also want to consider the resources your NFP partner has and how they could support the campaign. Here are some resources to think about:

1. *Celebrity ambassadors.* Sometimes, if the fit is right and the celebrity ambassador is open to it, there might be an opportunity to leverage one or more of the NFP's ambassadors.

2. *Brand ambassadors.* Many NFP organisations have people who volunteer and act as ambassadors for the organisation. They can sometimes be utilised during a campaign to represent the charity and to provide more information on the campaign and the charity brand to the customer.

3. *The CEO.* If the partnership is significant enough, there may be an opportunity to invite the NFP's CEO to your company to launch the campaign or the internal engagement part of the campaign. Alternatively, at the end of the campaign, inviting the CEO to receive the cheque for the fundraised amount can be effective and can deliver good PR.

Beyond your cause partner, there are often opportunities with other partners to your organisation. When there is a charitable drive happening, many partners are enthusiastic about getting involved to support your company's efforts in some way.

Airbnb's 'Until We All Belong' campaign (discussed earlier in Chapter 17) is a great example of leveraging partnerships. Because of a shared vision, Airbnb was able to unlock millions of dollars in media value through partners such as Qantas, ANZ, Google and Fairfax.

Below is a list of example partners you might want to consider as leverage or amplification opportunities for your campaign:

- Sponsorship partners
- Strategic partners who share your social vision or purpose
- Suppliers
- Other businesses that share your office building
- Cafés in or near the office building
- Media companies that operate media in your building – e.g. lift media.

The above list certainly isn't exhaustive. I recommend you mind-map all the potential partners and associated businesses that you could collaborate with to leverage your campaign.

CHAPTER 25

EVALUATION

Metrics are the lifeblood of any good marketer.

Too many marketing programs and campaigns today lack the meaningful metrics for evaluation that they need. Sometimes it's just too hard for marketers to get data that they can genuinely attribute to their marketing. Occasionally, though, I wonder if some marketers deliberately avoid hardcore evaluation metrics for their campaign, maybe out of a fear that it could reflect badly on them.

Sadly, I think this reflects on a company's leadership. Nowadays, there is such a strong focus on results that it becomes almost impossible for marketers to build a brand that people will value, beyond the latest 'what's in it for me?' grab. Perhaps that's contributed to the fact that people simply don't care about most brands today.

The nature of cause marketing will always bring sceptics and cynics out of the woodwork. Given that many people confuse CSR with cause marketing, there is all too often a perception that it is a waste of money that will achieve nothing beyond some woowoo worthiness or fluffy halos around the brand!

I hope the case studies I've shared with you in this book have established, beyond a doubt, the commercial value that cause marketing offers brands alongside the social value it delivers.

There is another argument – a traditionalist view that many in the social sector (and some outside of the sector) hold strongly. They believe that businesses have an obligation to contribute to society's interests and that they should be meeting that obligation without any expectation to profit out of it.

As you may have concluded, I disagree with that view. Everything I've written in this book contradicts that view. I wish we lived in a world where that traditionalist approach was enough, but it's not. The world is changing so quickly and our models and our worldview need to evolve with it – and fast, before we miss the wave of opportunity.

Governments worldwide are reducing funding to NFPs in response to budget pressures. As government contribution reduces, NFPs look towards businesses to increase their commitments. Meanwhile, businesses are facing their own challenges. Technology disruption has opened up competition from smaller, more agile organisations, and companies the world over have to reduce their operating costs. Restructures are a dime a dozen and budget cuts have become the new norm. Community and CSR budgets will find themselves on the frontline of these cuts as businesses redirect their investments to areas that drive the strongest ROI.

So, what are our options. Struggle on? Appeal to the business community's selfless sense of citizenship? Or take a realist view and move with the times?

I believe we stand at an exciting time where need meets opportunity. On one hand, we have the rise of Millennial citizens who want businesses to do more and brands to stand for something. On the other hand, we have brands needing to find new ways to reach consumers and to emotionally connect with them.

Social causes are the bridge between these two needs and marketing is the vehicle that makes it happen. Cause marketing or purpose-led marketing is the union of the two business functions of CSR and marketing.

Ultimately, if 'purpose' or cause marketing delivers strong tangible value to a business, the business will continue investing in it. If there's a case for it, it may even increase its investment.

It is therefore an absolute necessity to have a clear evaluation plan around your cause marketing program. It's not just to silence the critics. The purpose of evaluation, beyond the obvious, is to optimise your cause marketing program over time.

There are 11 key outcomes you need to be able to measure and they fall into the following four categories:

1. *Brand sociability:*
   - Media impressions
   - Social engagement
2. *Brand value, sales and ROI:*
   - Brand health
   - Sales increase
   - ROI
3. *Internal and stakeholder impact:*
   - Internal and partner engagement
   - Employee and stakeholder impact (net promoter score)
   - Anecdotal feedback

4. *Social impact:*
   - Social impact
   - Delivery on your social purpose or social impact goal
   - Social ROI.

Combined, these metrics will give a whole-picture view of the value of a cause or purpose-led marketing program to your business and will enable you to make the case for ongoing investment in your program. They will also highlight where there are opportunities for improvement, which will help you to optimise the program over time.

PART 4

MAKE MARKETING GREAT AGAIN

CHAPTER 26

FORTUNE FAVOURS THE BOLD

If you've read this book from the introduction and all the way through to here, then by now I hope you're convinced about the merits of cause marketing as a strategy that can enable you to achieve some critical outcomes for your brand. Given the many challenges the world faces, it's also way more than that. It's a commercially astute way for a business to become a part of the solution, mobilising your assets to create positive social impact. Finally, it's a realistic way for a brand to simply start on this path towards becoming a brand with purpose.

I hope this book has reshaped your perception of cause marketing from the very narrow tactical view that many in Australia still associate it with.

Here in Australia, we're fortunate to be at a reasonably early life stage of what I call 'cause marketing 2.0'. The first iteration of cause marketing was not a great start – a sea of pink products, many of them completely unrelated to the cause of breast cancer research or care. That was about 12 or so years ago and it was a brazen display of opportunism by many brands. Although this was not the case for all brands, for example, Mount Franklin has built a long-standing platform to fight against breast cancer, firstly by partnering with the National Breast Cancer Foundation (NBCF) and later through its partnership with the McGrath Foundation.

Today, brands approach cause marketing more cautiously, which is a good thing. A cause marketing program should be approached strategically and genuinely. It should be evaluated as a genuine desire to create impact as well as a long-term opportunity to unlock brand value. It is not just a short-term grab for sales.

I hope the case studies I've included in this book have provided you with some inspiration and ideas to take your first steps on a path to purpose.

A few years ago, I was having lunch with a client of mine. We've become friends over the years and I have a lot of respect for his opinion, so I shared something that was causing me frustration. I had spent the previous 12 months meeting with marketers and sharing research with them around the desire for brands to support good causes and some amazing case studies, similar to those in this book.

Smart brands will go beyond attention. They'll earn true followers, supporters and collaborators.

I explained to him that, without exception, the people I presented to loved the idea of cause marketing and got very excited about it and even inspired by it. But very few of them went on to take the next step to explore it as a genuine marketing solution for their brand. His response hit me hard.

He had extensive experience as a marketer in Australia across a diverse range of industries. He explained to me his observation, as a marketer in Australia, if you do the same thing you've always done and it doesn't work, nobody will have your head for it. But if you try something new and it doesn't work, you're mincemeat!

Fear – good, old fashioned fear – keeps many a good person down.

I'm not being judgmental. I get it. Too many Australian businesses don't empower their people to truly innovate – especially in big business. They may talk the game, but innovation inevitably means there are going to be some failures along the way. If a company doesn't allow for failure, then they're not allowing for innovation – not really.

But we live in times where innovation has become an imperative.

Technology disruption means the way people are consuming media has forever changed. Marketers now are forced to find new, better ways of engaging their audience. The old ways are simply no longer an option. Well, they are but you're pretty much guaranteed that investment in old-world marketing techniques is money down the drain.

Brands can't afford to use social media (heck, any media) to simply sell their wares. That one-way approach of 'you sit there while I tell you how great my brand is' is gone forever. Brands today need to earn people's attention. Smart brands will go beyond attention. They'll earn true followers, supporters and collaborators.

It's time to look forward. It's time to see your consumers as the citizens they are – a collaborator in action. It's time to do something cool in the world.

I'd like to end with a story.

I started my career in London in the early 1980s. I spent 10 years there and, at the time, I drove a little red Mazda MX5. It was a fun car, but not the most robust vehicle in the world. Anyone who has driven around Hyde Park Corner will know that it is the roundabout from hell. The amount of traffic going around it makes it nigh on impossible to get on it.

Too many times I found myself on the road leading in from Victoria, waiting for the smallest gap so I could accelerate onto the roundabout and almost every time, it seemed an impossible task. Meanwhile, I could sense the impatience of the car behind me, breathing down my neck, just wanting me to go.

There were a couple of times when I realised that waiting was no longer an option. Life was moving on and if I didn't as well, I would get left behind. So I did what any sensible person would do in that situation. I closed my eyes and accelerated, hoping and praying that I wasn't going to get ploughed into by the car careering around the corner.

Fortunately, I never got hit, nobody got hurt and everyone moved on their way.

The point is, there are many times in our lives when we become immobilised, whether by our own fear or that of others. Sometimes, you've just got to put your foot down on the accelerator and go. You've got to own your actions and hope for the best.

I've had many 'Hyde Park corner' moments in my life. I've had to take a leap of faith and hope for the best. Mostly, I've come out in good shape. There have been times when I've fallen on my face, but do you know what? I can barely remember them. So, I'm guessing they weren't all that important in the bigger scheme of things.

That's the funny thing about failure – you learn some great life lessons from it, which means that failure is actually just a path to success.

Ultimately, I believe what is most important is to keep moving. To be taking action of some kind and learning from each move.

When you look at the opportunities ahead, they're ridiculously exciting. Why wouldn't you want to grab them with both hands?

Today's the day to be bold, be true, have some fun along the way and to really and truly make your actions count.

As for fear... I saw a beautiful quote from Robin Sharma that sums it up perfectly:

> *'The fears we don't face become our limits. The opportunities we don't seize become our walls.'*

My wish is that you face down your most limiting fears and you go on to seize extraordinary opportunities.

CHAPTER 27

WELCOME TO THE CLUB

There are some incredible people in the world of cause and purpose-led marketing who are doing amazing things. Most of them are on a mission to build the profile and the value of cause marketing and release some great content. Here are some of the organisations and people that have been a great source of inspiration, motivation and guidance for me over the last few years as I've immersed myself in this subject.

ENGAGE FOR GOOD

www.engageforgood.com

Engage for Good (EFG) provides a treasure trove of information for businesses and non-profit organisations on creating successful corporate initiatives at the intersection of purpose and profit. Based in New York, its case studies, research and 'how to' content is skewed to the North American market but provides practical information that can be leveraged by cause marketers around the world. Particularly fascinating is its 15-year archive of programs that have won the group's coveted Halo Awards.

Founded in 2003 by David Hessekiel, a former journalist and marketing executive, EFG originally focused on largely promotional consumer-facing programs. Since David collaborated on the book *Good Works!* in 2012, EFG has expanded to cover such topics as employee engagement, behaviour change, cause promotion, corporate advocacy.

I've had the chance to attend EFG's annual conference, not once, but twice. It usually takes place at the end of May/early June and consists of two days of rubbing elbows and comparing notes with hundreds of professionals dedicated to creating successful cross-sector partnerships. It's a long trip, but I highly recommend it!

JOE WATERS SELFISH GIVING BLOG

www.selfishgiving.com/blog/

Joe's a friendly Bostonian who has been in the cause marketing business for more years than he'd probably like to admit to. His blog is an amazing resource for anyone interested in cause marketing. He's also the co-author of *Cause Marketing for Dummies*, which is available at Amazon.

CAUSE TALK RADIO PODCAST

www.engageforgood.com/resources/podcasts

Cause Talk Radio is a weekly podcast co-hosted by Megan Strand of Engage for Good and Joe Waters of *SelfishGiving.com*. Each 20-minute show explores a new trend, idea or discussion about a topic important to corporate and non-profit marketers with an emphasis on cause marketing.

CONSCIOUS CAPITALISM AUSTRALIA & NEW ZEALAND

Conscious Capitalism is a global movement, originating in the US, that now has spread across the world. The organisation was founded on the belief that business has the power to elevate humanity.

Australia was the first chapter to launch globally. In 2016, Conscious Capitalism Australia & New Zealand merged to bring together a community of business and thought leaders to co-create a movement of conscious business for the greater good.

If you are interested in the intersection of profit and purpose, I encourage you to sign up as a member. Not only will you get value out of it, you'll have the opportunity to contribute your own ideas. There are a range of membership options to suit individuals, students, businesses and corporations.

B1G1

www.b1g1.com

B1G1 is a global business-giving initiative on a mission to create a world full of giving. B1G1 makes it easy for businesses worldwide to make a positive impact by giving in unique and meaningful ways.

B1G1 is a global movement that makes a real impact on its business members and on our world. Currently, some 2,600 businesses form part of B1G1 and as of July 2017, they've created in excess of 111 million giving impacts around the world.

B1G1 uniquely links 'transactions' in your business with very carefully selected high-impact projects (currently there are over 600 of them) and it makes sure that 100 per cent of your giving flows directly to those projects. Better yet, your giving can start from just 1 cent.

For example, when you bought this book you made it possible to fund Khmer (Cambodian language) books for a month for five Cambodian girls.

It's a great example of the kind of giving-impacts that they enable for businesses of all sizes and from all kinds of industry background.

It means businesses with a real sense of purpose can change our world.

SHARED VALUE PROJECT

www.sharedvalue.org.au

The Shared Value Project is the peak practice body for shared value in Australasia and the exclusive regional partner of the Shared Value Initiative. The project drives the adoption and implementation of shared value strategies among leading companies, civil society and government organisations by providing thought leadership, knowledge and networks.

Through a program of workshops, training and events the Shared Value Project encourages individuals, organisations and change agents to view the creation of social value as a major competitive advantage, a driver of innovation and foundation for long-term economic prosperity.

B CORP

www.bcorporation.com.au

B Corp certification is to sustainable business what fair trade certification is to coffee. B Corp represents an emerging group of companies that are using the power of business to create a positive impact on the world and generate a shared and durable prosperity for all.

PUBLIC INC

www.publicinc.com

PUBLIC Inc. is a Canadian social impact agency and accelerator that helps brands profit with purpose. The agency believes the path to creating large scale social impact lies in merging social purpose with business benefit. Their clients include The Body Shop, Under Armour, Kruger and Maple Leaf Foods.

ALISOUN MACKENZIE FROM GIVE TO PROFIT

www.givetoprofit.com

Alisoun is a lovely Scottish lass who I met only recently when she was visiting Sydney. Our mutual interest in cause marketing brought us together. She has recently launched a book called *Give To Profit*. If you're a small-business owner or entrepreneur who likes to support social causes, this book shows you how to grow a profitable business and make a difference in the world at the same time. She's also planning to release a podcast in September 2017.

Buy on Amazon around the world at *www.bit.ly/givetoprofitus*.

BENOJO

www.benojo.com

Benojo provides the world's first social marketplace for good. Benojo is a marketplace that allows individuals, businesses and their employees, government and education sectors to promote and share offers of support to the charities and foundations they care the most about.

Similarly, charities and foundations can promote and share the support that they need. Benojo then takes care of the match-making and provides all the required tools to facilitate meaningful and sustainable relationships.

AN INVITATION TO CONNECT

Thank you for taking the time to read this book. I hope you got some value and inspiration from it. If you did then I'd like to invite you to connect with me.

Whether it's to talk about how you might take the next step or even if you'd like to discuss or debate some of the themes in this book, feel free to get in touch. If I can be of help in any way, I would love to hear from you.

One of the challenges I had when writing this book was in deciding which case studies and examples to share as I have so many. If I can help you move forward by sharing cause marketing examples that are more relevant to your category, I'd be happy to. Together we can achieve so much more than if we're feeling our way through new territory alone.

To anyone who goes on to implement a cause marketing strategy in their business, I'd like to say congratulations. I wish you every success in your efforts.

If you've enjoyed this book, please take a moment to give a review on Amazon and tell others about it.

Thank you.

WORK WITH CAROLYN

Sunday lunch is a brand consultancy specialising in cause, community and purpose-led marketing. We enable brands to do well by doing good. Our services include:

- *Discovery workshops* – Identify how a cause-led approach can work for your brand.
- *Purpose development workshops* – Develop a brand purpose that delivers a strong strategic foundation for brand development, differentiation and social impact.
- *Path to purpose program* – Implement the SIMPLE 6-step framework to cause-led marketing.
- *Fundraising programs* – For NFP organisations that want to develop fundraising programs, we offer consultancy services as well as full strategic, concept development and execution services.
- *Consulting* – Carolyn works with businesses on a consulting basis to help them develop and/or implement their cause-led marketing strategies.
- *Speaking* – Carolyn is available to speak about cause and purpose-led marketing.
- *Partnering* – Carolyn is interested in hearing about opportunities to partner and collaborate to further the cause and purpose-led movement.

To find out more, contact Carolyn at *www.sundaylunch.com.au* or *carolynbutlermadden.com*.

Lightning Source UK Ltd.
Milton Keynes UK
UKHW022030170321
380525UK00009B/2284